Bedtime Stories

For Corporate Executives

Tales to amuse and inspire leaders

Fernando Lanzer

Published with the support of
LCO Partners BV
Meester F. A. van Hallweg 23
1181ZT – Amstelveen
The Netherlands

Bedtime Stories for Corporate Executives

First printing October 2015

ISBN-10: 1515215334
ISBN-13: 978-1515215332

Text copyright © 2015 Fernando Lanzer Pereira de Souza
All Rights Reserved

Cover & back cover photography by
Jussara Pereira de Souza

Cover picture graphic design by
Bruna Pereira de Souza

Praise for "Take Off Your Glasses", also by Fernando Lanzer

"I find the book "Take Off Your Glasses" excellent, maybe the best common language explanation of my ideas that has been written so far."

Professor Geert Hofstede

"I think it is a great book, you are different because you really say what needs to be said. Many people are simply afraid to "rock the boat", especially here in the US, and this is why so many social and cultural fallacies keep being promoted and validated. I like very much the chapter The United States of Europe and the American Union."

Cosmin Gheorghe

"Thank you for passing this on. "Democracy in China" is the best article I have ever seen on Power Distance and clarified things for me too. I have lived in several countries with high Power Distance and found that this article summarized very well the attitudes of the citizens of these countries.
I agree with you that it is a timely reminder that we should be very wary of value judgments and there may be no such thing as "good" or "bad" on the culture scales, only "different". It is however extremely hard to reach this level of detachment, even when one understands the two cultures very well: we are all prisoners of our own cultural upbringing and education!"

Marvin Faure

Thank you for sending this, and I do really like it. It is the best (concise, clear, drily amusing) summary of Power Distance I have come across. I hope you don't mind, but I'm forwarding it on to people I know who are working with their clients on issues resulting from different perceptions of Power Distance.

Michael Newman

"By the way, I read and enjoyed your article on Democracy in China. It makes a lot of sense. I never saw things from the high/low PDI perspective. After living 30 years in Venezuela and observing the situation now, I can definitely see how ones culture and PDI have an impact on everything."

David Charner

"I read this with interest when you first sent it (and since visited China where I saw this at first hand!). However, it is all the more interesting now because I am in (southern) Italy running a course for 21 Mediterranean students from Syria, Egypt, Tunisia, Jordan, Iraq, Algeria and Palestine. The PDI concept within the current context of the Arab world is playing out in front of me every day with young, intelligent and engaging students. So too is it when I return to my room and watch BBC, Aljazeera, Press TV and CCTV. In all of these outlets it strikes me that the BBC has lost touch with the new reality as perhaps has the West in general. Thanks for sending me this excellent piece."

Sayed Azam-Ali

"Coming from Hong Kong, in spite of all the liberties I enjoy, I echo that power, privilege and responsibility are attached to positions. And I personally believe that it should stay this way here. In fact, I think that high power distance works better with capitalism given its meritocratic nature."

Victor Wong

"Thank you very much for sharing your article. It is very interesting and I agree with your insights. The democracy is differently working in China and it is working very well. The collective leadership in China has well planned succession plan and it works smoothly. They don't spend huge time and money for elections. Only one party dominates the politics, but they have pretty good plans to develop economy and society. There will be some mistakes and oppressing different opinions but they at least improved life of people significantly so far. I think they set up a good model for developing countries.
So, I realized later that different culture in developing countries will need different democracy system from western countries."

K. R. Yoon

Thanks for the book! I had a good laugh about Master Khard quoting the Beatles.

Geert Jan Hofstede

To my

family,

who told me stories

and taught me how to tell them

Contents

I - LEADERSHIP

1. The Answering Machine — 15
2. Bring Me My Red Shirt — 17
3. If I'm Not Quick — 19
4. Mosquito Musketeers — 21
5. Count Your Blessings — 23
6. The Firemen of Brumadinho — 25
7. Competing in the Desert — 27
8. The Old Rooster — 29
9. The Lady and the Politician — 31
10. Kissinger and the Trainee — 33
11. If You Can't Do It, You Teach — 35
12. Arthur Rubinstein — 37
13. Medicine for Memory — 39
14. Reincarnations of Jesus — 41
15. Mushroom Management — 43

II - DECISION MAKING

16. Executive Vacationing on a Farm — 47
17. Making the Best Decision — 49
18. A Recruiting & Selection Decision — 51
19. Sister Math and Sister Logic — 53
20. Lawyer Looking for a Parking Spot — 55
21. One Man, Three Whiskies — 57
22. Reducing a Big Issue in Size — 59

III - ORGANIZATIONAL CULTURE

23. The Bamboo Church — 63

24. The Family with a Cow	65
25. The Old Lady at the Doctor	67
26. A Spoon and a Chain Tied to Your Zipper	69
27. Two Statisticians Hunting Deer	71
28. The Good Rooster	73

IV - HIERARCHY

29. The Maestro	77
30. When You Look Up	79
31. When You Make a Huge Blunder	81
32. Three Parrots	83

V - MANAGING ACROSS BORDERS

33. The Game of Cachanga!	87
34. The Armadillo	89
35. Western Questions to a Chinese Professor	91
36. Reception in Peru	95
37. The Little German Boy Who Did Not Speak	97
38. Trapped in an Earthquake	99
39. Four People On A Train	101
40. The Survey In The Middle East	103
41. The Sheep In The Saloon	105
42. Dancing to the Music	107
43. Rabbi and Priest	109
44. Argentinian Expat in Spain	111
45. The Slobonian and the Matchboxes	113
46. Three Kinds of Hell	115
47. When Is It Corruption?	117
48. Bribing the Goalkeeper	121
49. Test Review at School	123
50. Malay, Chinese & Indian on Gates of Heaven	127
51. British Drinking Water in India	129
52. Learning in a Hierarchical Culture	131
53. Dinner Without Speaking the Language	133

54. Two Nationalities in a Cruise Ship	135
55. Know-how and Savoir-faire	137

VI - LEARNING

56. The Speed Of Light	141
57. Cavalry Recruits	143
58. Three Nuns at the Pearly Gates	145
59. Englishman Training a Camel	147
60. Teaching a Dog to Pee Outside	149
61. Detailed Instructions	151
62. Chinese Speaking Yiddish	153
63. The Difference: Psychologists & Psychiatrists	155
64. Missing the Flight	157

VII - CAREER DEVELOPMENT

65. At The Zoo	161
66. Engineer In a Monkey Costume	163
67. Killing a Lion Each Day	165
68. A story with Three Morals	167
69. Rabbit Succession	169

VIII - CHANGE MANAGEMENT

70. Psychology and Change	173
71. The Old Man With the Coat	175
72. Consultant to Oedipus Rex	177

ACKNOWLEDGMENTS	181
REFERENCES	183
ABOUT THE AUTHOR	185

Foreword

I've used the stories in this book in coaching, lectures, presentations and workshops that I've led throughout a long career. They have served to illustrate certain aspects of what I was trying to communicate, most of the time. In some occasions, they were used simply to create a lighter atmosphere about some very serious issues.

I am a firm believer in the power of humor to help get messages across. I do acknowledge that many of these stories are not "Politically Correct"; however, I hope this will not stop you from enjoying them. I apologize in advance if anyone may feel offended by these tales; my intention is to amuse and inspire, perhaps even to provoke thought and reflection, along with a smile. I bear no ill wishes to any of the several ethnic groups mentioned, especially to the Slobonians, whom I admire and respect.

I often make fun of those leaders who behave like some of the characters in the book's jokes, pretending to be something they are not. Many stories in this book are similar in this aspect: they portray characters that are misbehaving, but the intention in telling such tales is to criticize that behavior through humor. That is also how I have often used them in my professional practice: as a comic anecdote about what NOT to do.

My target audience is corporate executives and all those who might be interested in using these stories to make a point or illustrate a concept. This might include basically anyone interested in the topics these anecdotes address.

Corporate executives are people, contrary to what you may read on political militant writings all over the world. I was one of them, a while ago, (actually, I was first a militant and later an executive) and became an executive coach and consultant to many senior leaders in the past ten years. In my experience, I've seen how they can suffer from the "loneliness at the top" syndrome; I've identified with them and I've felt sorry for them, as they are often dedicated and unselfish people striving to make things work and reach ambitious goals in order to obtain the elusive approval of others (shareholders, clients, staff, regulators, pundits).

These stories are meant to give corporate executives some comfort as they wind down at the end of the day and prepare to sleep. My intention is that many readers will read sections of this book in bed, just before turning out the lights. I hope the stories will inspire them for the work they will face on the next morning; perhaps they will use some of these tales as an opening joke during a presentation to the Supervisory Board or at a shareholder's meeting. I trust the stories may be useful and that they might allow executives to drift off to sleep with a smile on their faces.

PART I – LEADERSHIP

1. The Answering Machine

In his book "Leading Out Loud", Terry Pearce tells the story about a friend of his who had an unusual message on his answering machine. If you would call him and he wasn't home, the message you would hear would be something like this:

"Hi, this is not an answering machine, it's a questioning machine; and I have two questions for you: who are you and what do you want?" After a small pause, the message continues:

"You may think that these are trivial questions, but consider the fact that most people go through their entire lives trying to answer these two questions…"

Indeed these are very powerful questions. If there is one thing that I would like people to take away from my coaching sessions or from the workshops I run, it is to keep these two questions on their minds, always… And to spend their lives addressing the changing answers that they can provide to these two questions, as they grow and evolve as human beings and as leaders.

2. Bring Me My Red Shirt!

Courage is an attribute often cited as being a requirement for effective leaders. To introduce the topic, I have many times used this story, which also illustrates how it is important to appear bold and courageous to your team, even if you might not be feeling so brave inside.

There once was a merchant ship, in the 17th Century, much akin to a corporation in the 21st Century, with a CEO and all, only that in those days the CEO was called "Captain". This ship was sailing back to the Head Office, full of valuable commodities taken from the colonies to increase shareholder value back home, when the otherwise peaceful journey was disturbed by a frantic shout from the lookout perch atop the main mast:

"Captain! I see pirates approaching quickly from the starboard side!"

The Captain quickly assesses the situation with a couple of special advisors, and concludes that the pirate ship is much faster than his own, loaded with commodities and heavy debentures; there is no way to avoid the pirates closing in and going for a very hostile takeover.

He shouts to his crew: "Battle stations, everyone! Prepare to fight!" And, turning to his Personal Assistant: "Bring me my red shirt!"

The Captain dons his red shirt and leads his men courageously into battle. After an epic struggle, they manage to win the fight and send the pirates away, scuttling off to tend to their wounded.

The whole crew yells in celebration and the Captain orders an extra ration of rum for everyone.

As the crew sing and dance and drink into the night, his PA approaches the Captain with a question, in private: "Sir, why did you ask for your red shirt, just before the fighting began?"

The Captain adopts a brave posture, gazing into the horizon, and reveals: "It was for the benefit of our crew's morale! If I were to be wounded in battle, I did not want my men to see my bleeding wounds, lest they might feel discouraged from continuing to fight!"

The PA is moved by this lesson in Leadership, and notes it down in his diary, which he intends to someday get published as "From Great to Greater: Lessons From A Leader Ship".

The journey continues uneventfully for another week, until peace is again broken by a shout from the lookout perch:

"Captain! I see the pirates coming back again! And this time they've brought reinforcements, I see five pirate ships approaching fast from the starboard side!"

The Captain yells: "Battle stations, everyone!" And to his PA across the deck: "Bring me my brown trousers!"

3. If I'm Not Quick...

A good leader must often appear to be right, even when he might appear to be wrong. This may not be such a truthful axiom, but many people believe in it... They strive to maintain appearances, even when facing very adverse outcomes.

This is illustrated by the story told about a Uruguayan agriculture technician. The background to this is that Uruguay is a very small country in South America, with an economy based on agriculture and on raising cattle and sheep. It is surround by the two most powerful economies in the continent: Brazil and Argentina. It was able to maintain its independent status during the 19th Century basically due to support from the UK, as a kind of buffer zone between the two larger South American rivals.

Naturally, the Uruguayans are a proud people; they have to be, in order to face up to the very real threat of being swallowed by any of their two much bigger neighbors. They've earned a reputation for never admitting defeat, even when the facts point otherwise. This has enabled them to obtain important victories against all odds, in sports and in business negotiations. The country has invested historically in the education of its small population, so the general education level is higher than that of their neighbors, and many Uruguayans become successful immigrants both in Brazil and in Argentina, because of their expertise, and since there are more job opportunities in the larger economies of their neighbors.

As the story goes, this agriculture technician works as a consultant to many farms and ranches across the border in Brazil. His advice does add value to his clients' farming practices, though they are sometimes annoyed by his "I'm better than you are, and I'm always right" attitude.

One client who is particularly annoyed by this guy decides to play a trick on him, taking advantage of the fact that the Uruguayan knows a lot about raising crops, but practically zilch about horses and cattle, though of course never admitting to not knowing everything about everything.

During one of the consultant's visits to his farm, our client guy asks the specialist for some advice about a mule, who seems to have some kind of problem in one of its hind legs. The Uruguayan would never admit to not knowing anything about mules, so he agrees to take a look.

Now, the first thing you learn about handling mules is to never approach them from behind: they don't like that, and tend to react with a very powerful kick, sure to knock out whoever is on the receiving end.

The client, counting on the Uruguayan's ignorance, asks him to approach the mule from behind, bend down and take a close look at the mules left leg.

As the technician does just that, and bends down with his head practically on the mule's ass, the mule delivers a direct blow to his forehead and throws him three meters back against the barn wall.

People rush to pick the guy up, with a horseshoe shape stamped across his forehead. Dazed, cross-eyed and about to faint, he manages to blurt out: "Wow! If I'm not quick, that would have caught me in the eye!"

So, no matter how stupid you've been, never admit it! Specially if you are leading a team of Uruguayans...

4. Mosquito Musketeers

The Three Musketeers, characters created by Alexandre Dumas, were famous not because of their muskets, but because of their swordsmanship... In this old tale, an Uruguayan musketeer meets a Spaniard to compete and determine who is the best swordsman.

Similarly to the tale on Chapter 3, another Uruguayan, back in the 18th Century, was involved in a competition with a famous Spanish swordsman, visiting the local branch from the Head Office in Madrid.

They started bragging about their skills in a bar, each one telling ever more outrageous stories about their swordsmanship achievements.

Eventually, the Spaniard rose to his feet and proposed a way to end the discussion by proving, in practice, who was the best, the quickest and most accurate.

He quickly grabbed a mosquito that was flying around. He held it in his hand and drew his sword. He then addressed everyone who had gathered around them to hear the bragging stories.

"Now, watch carefully, gentlemen"

He released the mosquito in the air and, with a single swift movement of his sword, split in two, right in the air.

An "Ooohh!" of amazement spread through the small crowd.

Never to be outdone, the Uruguayan also grabbed a mosquito that was flying around, although with a bit more difficulty than the Spaniard.

He also held it in his hand, drew his sword and addressed the group of people around them.

"Now watch!" he whispered, creating suspense.

He released the mosquito in the air and moved his sword just as swiftly as the Spaniard had done, but the mosquito continued to fly around unfazed...

The Uruguayan shouted: "Te irás, te irás, pero hijos jamás tendrás!" (Go on, get out of here, but you will never have children!)

With a single stroke, he had castrated the mosquito!

The lesson here is to claim that you have done something amazing, even when you actually have failed to achieve what you intended in the first place.

Of course, I say this in jest. As an author, I am not advocating that people should do this in real life (especially the part about mutilating mosquitoes...).

5. Count Your Blessings

Leadership requires being comfortable with who you are and passionate about what you want. This also means being content with what you have, counting your blessings, even though you may always wish for more.

At a cocktail party thrown by a major investment bank, a young banker was amused by an old man that he saw in a corner of the ballroom, drink in hand, smiling effusively all the time. He decided to approach him, out of curiosity.

"Hi, I'm Patrick Bateman," he introduced himself. "I'm with Pierce & Pierce."

"Good to meet you, Patrick. I'm Robert Longfellow, retired. Used to work for Lehmann, a long time ago."

"I noticed you smiling all the time… What are you so happy about?"

"Well, you know, son? I'm 82 now, and the age is getting to me. When I was your age, I used to have sex every night, sometimes two or three times on the same night! Then, as the years went by, I couldn't do it as often. I did it two times a week, then once a week. After a while, I only did it once a month. And nowadays, I can only do it once a year…"

"I'm sorry, that's actually pretty sad… So why are you smiling so much?"

"Because it's tonight, my boy! It's tonight!"

To be an effective leader, you need to be able to show the way and inspire others to follow your ideas. In order to be an inspiring individual, you need to be authentic, at ease with yourself, content with what you have achieved, and optimistic. People are eager to follow those who show confidence and a positive attitude. Rather than complain about your condition, count your blessings and show the world that you can do more and enjoy doing it, too.

6. The Firemen of Brumadinho

At the beginning of the 1930's there was a big fire in the small Portuguese village of Beiras Altas. The firemen couldn't put it out and the fire was spreading to other houses, threatening to burn down the whole town. The mayor called the neighboring villages and offered a cash prize of €1,000 to anybody who could come and help put out the fire. The neighboring village of Brumadinho, for instance, had a fire truck, and that could make a real difference in this dire situation.

The Brumadinho firemen responded as quickly as they could. They got on their old fire truck and drove it immediately to Beiras Altas, sirens blazing.

As they entered the village there were many people on the streets trying to put out the fire, but the fire truck did not stop: it cut through the crowd at high speed and drove right smack into the middle of the blaze, drawing a gasp of amazement from the people around.

The firemen jumped out of the truck with fire hoses spurting water in all directions. They managed to split the fire in two different blazes, and by doing this, the two fires became smaller and soon everyone could help to bring them down and put them out.

The mayor congratulated them for their strategy and thanked them, handing them a check for €1,000. The local radio station news reporter came to interview the fire captain live at the scene.

"This is fantastic", said the reporter, "thank you for saving our village! And what are you going to do with the prize money?"

"Well," replied the captain, "the first thing we'll do is get new brakes for the fire truck!"

This story illustrates how sometimes brave deeds occur by chance, not by choice… Should praise be withheld, when this happens? Something to ponder, depending on circumstances.

7. Competing in the Desert

In a war in the Middle East, a United Nations peace-keeping force was formed with soldiers from many different nations.

One day a caravan of soldiers going through the desert got hit by a huge sandstorm. As a result of that, people got lost, vehicles went in different directions and when the storm was over, there were three soldiers stranded in the middle of nowhere, with no food and no water. They were an American, a Russian and a Mexican.

They walked together for three days and couldn't find anything; they were really in bad shape. Suddenly, they found an old jeep, half-buried in the sand. They ran to it, hoping to find food or water, but all they found was a bottle of Coca Cola. They started fighting amongst themselves for it, until the American shouted: "Wait! Let's settle this in a civilized way! Let's organize a competition, and whoever wins, gets the bottle of Coke as a prize."

Americans, of course, are always keen to organize competitions...

"OK", said the Russian. "Let's do a long-distance jump. Whoever can leap the longest, gets the Coca-Cola."

They all agreed. The American drew a takeoff line on the sand, the Russian started to stretch his muscles in preparation, the Mexican sat down and watched.

The American was the first to go. He took some distance, ran to the takeoff line and jumped. The Russian took a measure tape from his backpack and measured the jump: four and a half meters. Not bad, considering the world record is almost nine meters.

Next came the Russian. He raised his eyes to the sky in a silent prayer, ran like crazy to the takeoff line and jumped... Four meters and seventy-five! He beat the American, with an impressive leap.

Then it was the Mexican's turn. He made a cross-sign on his chest, murmured a prayer to the Virgin of Guadalupe, ran to the takeoff line, tripped and fell flat on his face in the sand.

The other two ran to him shouting. "That was no jump! That was pathetic! Come on, can't you do better than that? Get up, we'll let you try again."

The Mexican writhed on the ground, holding his belly: "It's because I just had a bottle of warm Coke..."

This story was once told to me by a Mexican friend, illustrating how proud he was of a mindset that values being smart, more than being disciplined to comply and compete observing standard rules that might put you at a disadvantage. In some cultures, this behavior might be perceived as utterly despicable and be completely rejected; in other cultures, this is a source of pride.

A character (a Mexican police officer) in the Mel Gibson movie "Get The Gringo" speaks a great line to his American counterpart, a Border Patrol police officer:
"My friend: you are corrupt, we are corrupt; but at least we're honest about it!"

8. The Old Rooster

Sometimes an old timer can still be of some use, despite his or her age. This story is popular with those over 50.

There once was a young city slicker who became fed-up with the stress of living in New York City; he decided to quit investment banking and go live in the country. After cashing in on his last multi-million dollar bonus on Wall Street, he bought himself a piece of land in Ohio and moved there to become a farmer. He wanted to keep his farm small and just enjoy the simple life. He started raising chickens and pigs, planted some corn and took it easy.

Everything was going just fine, but one of the things he noticed was that his chickens laid a lot of eggs, but they never hatched any chicks. He asked some advice from a neighboring farmer.

His neighbor burst out laughing: "That's because you don't have a rooster, boy! You ain't ever gonna get any chicks unless you get yourself a rooster to cover them! That's what roosters are for!"

"OK," said the rookie farmer. "And where can I get a rooster? Do you have one to sell me?"

"Well, I don't have a rooster to sell ya… But I got one that you can borrow for a week, until you find one that you can buy. It's old Cockeye, been with me for some years now. I call him Cockeye 'cause he lost an eye in a fight with another rooster some time ago. He was getting old, so I got myself a young rooster a couple of months ago. On his first day in the chicken coop, the young'un beat the crap out of old Cockeye. Sure showed him who's the new boss… Now he won't even let Cockeye come near the chickens, let alone cover them… So Cockeye just wanders around in the farm, away from the chicken coop … Hasn't had any chicks for six weeks now. But I suppose he could still be of some use to ya, especially if he doesn't have to fight for territory with another rooster."

The new farmer looked at Cockeye, at the far end of the yard. He was limping a bit, and looked skinny and battered. It didn't seem likely that he would be capable of doing much; he could barely walk… But it wouldn't hurt to give it a try. "Sure, I'll take him and give him a chance. I'll return him in a week. By then I should have found one that I can buy and keep on a permanent basis. Meanwhile, Cockeye can be my interim manager."

"Intra what?" asked the old farmer.

"Never mind," said the rookie. "Just put him in a cage and hand him over."

When the young farmer got to his farm, Cockeye saw all those sexy spring chickens parading about and went crazy. He started rattling his cage and let out a horny "Cockadoodle-do!" When the farmer let old Cockeye loose, he was raring to go. After all, he hadn't been near a chick in six weeks! And watching pictures of prize chicks on The Farmer's Almanac was just not enough for him to get his rocks off.

He jumped on the closest chick and did her, then the next, and started chasing after every chicken in the yard. The farmer was pleased and went inside the house to catch up on his reading of "Take Off Your Glasses". Throughout the whole afternoon, he could hear the ruckus that Cockeye was stirring up in the yard. It sounded as if he was going to get every one of the two-dozen chickens on the farm.

Then, just before sunset, suddenly there was a deep silence. The farmer found that odd after all the noise that had been going on and he went out to the yard to see what was happening.

He found old Cockeye stretched out like a corpse in the middle of the yard. It looked like the stress had been too much for him. He had gotten all the chicks, all right, but that was the end of him. Already a buzzard was circling over his motionless body, slowly moving downwards in a spiral.

The farmer walked over somberly, thinking, "Shit, what am I going to tell my neighbor? He was so fond of old Cockeye... I suppose I just better bring him the old rooster's body before it gets dark..."

But as he bent down to pick up Cockeye's skinny corpse, the rooster whispered to him from the corner of his beak: "Shit, get out of here... I'm gonna get that blackie swooping down on me and you're scaring her off!"

The moral in this story is that older, experienced managers can often surprise you and do much more than you expect. Don't be so quick to discount them!

9. The Lady and the Politician

This story was once told by a Latin American Presidential candidate at a formal dinner. Some of the American feminists were not impressed, but most of the audience appreciated it.

It is very important, when you go into politics, especially in Latin America, to understand the difference between a lady and a politician. Do you know what that is?
When a lady says no, she means maybe; when she says maybe, she means yes; and when she says yes, then she is not a lady!
For a politician, it is quite different.
When a politician says yes, he means maybe; when he says maybe, he means no; and when he says no, then he is not a politician!

The story illustrates the codification of language in different culture situations. In practice, the meaning of the messages we communicate is not restricted to actual content; it is always codified and acquires special meaning when the context is taken into account. This is even more relevant in Collectivist cultures such as most Latin American, African and Asian cultures; Individualist cultures such as the ones found in Northern Europe and in the US tend to put more emphasis on content, rather than context, but it's just a matter of degree and intensity. Context is always there, adding meaning to content. Context has different meanings in different cultures; and that is why the same sentence (content) may have very different meanings in different cultures!

This also explains why some of the stories in this book may be considered hilarious in some cultures, and very offensive in others.

10. Kissinger and the Trainee

They say that many years ago, when Henry Kissinger was secretary of state, he got a young management trainee that was very talented and eager to please.

One Wednesday afternoon he called the trainee into his office and asked him: "I need a paper analyzing the situation in the Middle East. Can you write one for me?"

"Sure!" said the eager trainee.

"Good. Hand it in by close of business Friday."

On Friday afternoon the trainee gave Kissinger the paper, which he added to a pile of work he was taking home for the weekend.

On Monday morning Kissinger called the trainee into his office. As the trainee walked in expectantly, Kissinger held the paper out to him and asked: "Is this the best you can write on the situation in the Middle East?"

"Well," stuttered the trainee, "you only gave me a couple of days... If I had more time, I'm sure I could do more research on the subject..."

"Fair enough," said Kissinger. "Take it and re-write it. You have the whole week until Friday".

The trainee took the paper and spent the whole week researching and writing it again. On Friday, he gave it to Kissinger, who stuffed it again in his "work for home" briefcase.

On Monday morning Kissinger called the trainee into his office again and asked: "Are you sure that this is the best you can do about the Middle East?"

The trainee was surprised: "This is a good analysis about the political situation, but I didn't look at the culture angle, or the long term history of the region..."

"Then take it and re-write it again. I'll give you another week."

This time the trainee really put his whole heart and mind into the task. He worked through the night; he researched every possible source of information.

On Friday he again handed in the paper, exhausted but pleased with what he had accomplished.

On Monday Kissinger called the trainee into his office for the third time. He had the same inquiring expression on his face as he asked: "Are you quite sure that this is absolutely the best report you can write to me about the Middle East?"

"Yes!" exclaimed the trainee. "This is the best report anybody could possibly write on the Middle East! I looked at every possible angle, I made the deepest possible analysis. This is definitely the best report I could write!"

"Good," said Kissinger. "Then I will read it."

This story illustrates the power of constructive challenge. Kissinger never said the report was bad; he simply questioned whether the trainee was really doing the best he could. And it was the trainee's own sense of self criticism that led him to improve the report every time he was questioned, until he was absolutely sure that he had really done the best that he possibly could.

11. If You Can't Do It, You Teach It

They say that if you are incompetent to do something, you become a manager; if you're not able to manage the subject, then you become a teacher of the subject; if you cannot teach it, then you write a book about it; and if you cannot write well, then you become a consultant... That's how people become consultants!

I've often used this as a bit of self-deprecating humor. This, of course, goes down better in some cultures (for instance: Dutch) and not so well in other cultures (for instance: Italian). That depends on how important it is, in a given culture, to maintain a positive image of yourself at all times.

Usually, cultures that value academic achievement and theoretical exponentials, such as the French and the Germanic cultures, tend to flinch at making fun of university professors and writers; cultures that are more pragmatic and action-oriented, such as the British and the American, tend to rather enjoy making fun of academics and theorists.

12. Arthur Rubinstein and the Snowstorm

This is a story I have often used when facing an unexpectedly small audience. For all kinds of reasons, sometimes audiences for lectures or workshops are much smaller than expected. This usually elicits a feeling of awkwardness, both in the presenter and in the members of the audience themselves.

Rather than sulk about it, or simply pretend to ignore the awkward feeling, I prefer to acknowledge what is going on, but do it in a humorous way, by starting the session with the following story.

Many years ago the great classical pianist Arthur Rubinstein, already in his seventies, was touring the Northern United States in the winter. He arrived at a town in Michigan just as a snowstorm hit the place. He spent the night at a hotel that was just across the street from the theater where he was due to perform in the evening of the next day.

It snowed heavily during the whole night and also throughout the day. When it was time for him to cross the street to the theater, he had to be carried over by two staff members of the company organizing the concert, through snow that was three feet deep.

The organizers thought of cancelling the event. The tickets had already been sold out for days, but nobody would be able to get through the snow and reach the theater, they thought.

Rubinstein peeked through the curtains and saw that there was one man sitting in the audience, alone by himself. Somehow, that person had made it, braving through the terrible weather. This was surely the tiniest audience Rubinstein had ever played for; but having the highest professional standards, he felt that he should certainly perform for this single man in the audience, with the same dedication that he would play for a full house.

At precisely 7 pm, according to the program, the curtains opened and Rubinstein appeared on stage. The man in the audience stood up and clapped effusively.

Rubinstein bowed slightly, looked at him and said: "Before I start, I would like to thank you for making the huge effort to face the storm, and for being here tonight."

The man replied. "No need to thank me, Sir. I wouldn't miss this opportunity for anything in the world. I've always wanted to hear you sing!"

This addresses the frustrated expectations from both the presenter and the audience, when there is a small attendance, regarding the fact that everyone would prefer to be there together with many more people than just the few that are actually present. And yet, the situation is what it is, so the best thing to do is to make the best of it. One can only hope that the presentation will be satisfactory, and that other expectations of those who are present in the audience will not be frustrated…

13. Medicine for Memory

Two elder executives are chatting at a friend's dinner party, drinks in hand, standing next to a window, just before moving to the dining table.

One of them says: "You know, the worst part of getting older is that my memory is no longer what it used to be. When I was younger, I could remember details of every report I read, I could quote our sales figures from last year on the spot. I can't do that anymore without having to look up the numbers."

The other replies: "You know, I was having the same problem, but my wife talked me into seeing this doctor, and he gave me this medicine that is really making me remember things better, you should try some yourself. Now what's the name of the medicine again?..."

He scratches his head, makes an effort to remember, but to no avail. He looks at his friend and asks: "Help me out: what's the name of a flower... a red flower... with thorns on the stem?"

"You mean a rose?..." *his friend replies, tentatively.*

"Yes!" *And, turning to his wife:* "Rose, what's the name of that medicine I'm taking, again?"

This is a nice story to mention whenever the theme is older executives, people getting older, or the fact that your memory may fade as you get older. The subject may be considered as a delicate one, to some people under certain circumstances, so you need to assess the situation and determine whether it is appropriate to approach the issue in a light-hearted way, in order to ease eventual tensions around it, or if you should simply avoid it completely.

Try not to forget these tips, on when to use the story...

14. Reincarnations of Jesus

The Vatican got word that three different people were going about claiming that they were each actually a reincarnation of Jesus Christ. One of them was a German, the other a Frenchman, and the third was a Dutchman.

The Catholic Church does not take these things lightly, so they formed a committee of cardinals to look into the matter and go visit each of the three men, with the purpose of assessing whether there might be any truth to what they were claiming.

The group went first to Germany and met the claimant on the margins of the Rhein River. The German announced to them: "Behold! I can walk on water!" He proceeded to walk across the river until he got to the other side, barely getting his feet wet.

Some onlookers were quite amazed and immediately got to their knees and prayed; but the cardinals were skeptical. "I don't know," said one of them. "This whole thing seems to have been well prepared in advance…"

"Yes," said another one. "He brought us to this specific spot. Maybe he knows of a path stepping on stones just beneath the waters." They concluded that this was not enough evidence to prove this man was the reincarnation of Jesus.

The committee proceeded to Paris, where they met the Frenchman at a café on the Champs Elysées. "Behold!" said the Frenchman. "Free bread and wine for all!" A crowd soon gathered around him. He sat down with them at a table on the sidewalk and started distributing pieces of bread and pouring wine for all. And no matter how many people came, there was always enough bread and enough wine for everyone. It seemed like a real miracle!

Still, the cardinals were not impressed. "I don't know," said one of them. "There were so many people around us that we couldn't see what was really going on…" "Indeed", said another one. "There could be someone sneaking bread and wine for him from the kitchen. In the confusion, in the midst of such a large crowd, we would never notice that." They concluded that this man's claim could not be ascertained to be true.

Next, the committee went to Amsterdam to meet the Dutch guy. He took them to the Red Light District and went straight to one of their famous windows. He knocked. A prostitute opened the door and exclaimed: "Jesus! You again?!"

Religion is also a subject that needs to be treated carefully, so you need to think about your audience before deciding to tell this story. However, bear in mind that the Dutch are quite open to self-deprecating humor (it was a Dutchman who originally told me this story).

I've used it to illustrate how leaders sometimes make bold claims, which they are later asked to substantiate, either to the general public or to a Board of Directors (akin to the committee of cardinals in the story). If you find yourself in a similar situation, make sure you can impress your audience better than these three guys impressed the cardinals!

15. Mushroom Leadership Style

They say that many managers still practice the old leadership style referred to as "the mushroom style of leadership": "keep them in the dark and feed them shit; and whoever sticks their head out, chop it off!"

The term was coined by unhappy staff members who complained that their manager (or managers) never gave them any information about what was really going on. In the rare occasions that these managers told them something, it was usually something false or "corporate bullshit."

These managers are also known to be afraid of any rising talent who might cast a shadow over them, or threaten to take over their position in the future. Therefore, they discourage staff members who stand out, who show leadership skills or who simply perform above average, labeling them as "show-offs" that are trying to challenge their own position.

By doing so, they often alienate their best people. As word gets around, both inside the company and out in the labor market, they find it harder and harder to attract talent to join their teams.

PART II – DECISION MAKING

16. Executive Vacationing on a Farm

Once upon a time there was an executive who after 20 years at a large corporation, the last 5 of them as part of the Top Management Team, suddenly felt that he was on the brink of a nervous breakdown. He decided to take a three-month sabbatical period and asked his uncle Donald whether it was okay for him to spend some time with him at his farm, far from the madding crowd in New York.

The uncle welcomed him with open arms. For the first three days the executive simply slept like he never had done before. At last he could really relax and take his mind off corporate issues. He could just sit around and do nothing, take long naps, breathe in the pure countryside air, enjoy the silence seldom disturbed by cattle mooing in the distance.

After three days of this, however, he began to get a little restless. He just was not used to spending so much time doing nothing. He asked his uncle if there was anything he could do around the farm to help out.

His uncle said: "Well, things here in the farm are very different from what you are used to doing in them fancy offices in Manhattan... To tell you the truth, I don't know if there's anything here that needs doing that you would know how to do!"

"That's not a problem," said the executive. "Just give me a chance to prove that I'm up to it, let me try. I can do anything."

The uncle took his cap off and thought for a second or two. "Hmm," he said. I've got about 50 chickens to kill and take to the wholesale distributor. Can you chop their heads off and put them on the truck?"

"Sure," said the executive, happy with having a goal to achieve and a challenge to overcome. "Just point me in the right direction."

Well before supper time the executive told his uncle that the task was all done and the chickens were loaded on the truck and ready to go. The uncle was pleasantly surprised.

The next day, the executive was up early and eager to do something else. His uncle gave him the assignment to fertilize a whole field that had just been planted; he had to get a wagon-load of manure sitting in the barn and spread it out over a large field.

This was hard work and it took him the whole day; but by the end of the afternoon he had done it all and was pleased to announce his task was accomplished. The uncle complimented him on a job well done.

On the next day the executive was up early again and eager to get started on something else. This time the uncle took him to the barn and showed him a big pile of potatoes in a corner: "I've got all these potatoes that I have to take to the retailers at the market tomorrow. The thing is, I can get a better price if I put them in different bags according to size. I need you to sort them out in three sizes: small, medium and large; and then put them in different bags according to size. Got it?"

"Sure," said the executive. "This is easy enough, I'll be done in a jiffy!"

The uncle went off to do other chores and, after a couple of hours, returned to the barn to see how the executive was doing. To his surprise, he found the executive standing by the potato pile with a few potatoes in his hands. All the bags were empty. As he stepped nearer, the farmer heard the executive talking to himself: "Let's see... this is a small potato, and this is a medium one; now this next one is smaller than the second one, so it should actually be a medium;... but that means the other one should be a large, instead of a medium... but then this other one is even larger, so the previous one has to be medium..."

The uncle asked: "What happened? You didn't even get started?"

"Let's face it," responded the executive. "I'm no good at this! I can chop heads off and I can spread the shit around, but I just can't make decisions!"

This story pokes fun at the fact that making decisions is difficult, perhaps the most difficult aspect of being a manager. It can also be used to illustrate how important it is in America to be a decisive manager. Indeed, if you have difficulty making decisions you will have great difficulty as a manager in the United States, for this is one of your primary responsibilities.

17. Making the Best Decision

Making the right decision is often a matter of perspective, as this story illustrates:

A Slobonian (a fictitious nationality, conveniently used to replace any nationality of people that might be offended, if you used them to represent nationals who are regarded as stupid or "intelligence challenged." Depending on how Politically Correct you want to be, you might use it in all your ethnic jokes, or replace it with the nationality that you most enjoy making fun of...) ran into another Slobonian driving a pink, convertible Cadillac.

He asked him to pull over and, after exchanging greetings, expressed his surprise: "Hey man, what are you doing driving around in that car? That's a lady's car, man!"

"I know," smiled his friend. "You'll never believe what just happened to me! A couple of months ago I lent some $5,000 dollars to a sexy blond that came to my office. She was supposed to pay me back in a week, but she didn't. I called her several times and she kept stalling me and giving all kinds of lame excuses. So I threatened her and went to her house to collect. When she saw me coming, she hopped into this pink Cadillac and drove away. So I went after her. She drove out of town and tried to shake me off, but I kept following her. Eventually she drove into a dirt road in the middle of the woods and still I followed her. Finally, it turned out to be a dead end road. She was cornered.

She got out of the car, took all her clothes off, raised her arms and told me: 'Look, I don't have your money; I can't pay you back. Take what you want!'

So I took the car and left!"

"You're a smart guy!" said the first Slobonian. "Her clothes would not have fitted you!"

This story may be criticized, eventually, by feminists, so I would not advise you to tell it at the NOW (National Organization for Women) annual convention... Unless you happen to be Slobonian.

18. A Recruiting & Selection Decision

This story might be told to illustrate how large corporations should rely on psychologists to help them make hiring decisions.

The CEO of a large corporation asked his Human Resources Director to hire him a new executive secretary. After looking through dozens of CV's and interviewing several candidates, the search was narrowed down to three candidates, who were all highly qualified. The HR director came to the CEO's richly decorated office, accompanied by the Company Psychologist.

"These three candidates are all highly qualified and we have basically a tie among the three," said the HR director, laying the three dossiers with pictures of the three candidates on the CEO's mahogany desk in front of him. "You would do well to choose any of the three as your secretary; but I brought along Mr. Goodscores, our Corporate Psychologist, to assist you in making your decision."

"OK, so what's your advice?" asked the CEO to Mr. Goodscores.

"Well, it was difficult to choose among the three, so I decided to ask them a final, simple question at the end of each interview. I asked them: 'How much is two and two?'"

The first candidate said simply 'Two and two is four!' Her response shows that she is straightforward and reliable.

The second candidate hesitated for a second and then said 'two and two is twenty two!' This tells us that she is creative and can look behind appearances to find a deeper meaning to things.

The third candidate thought it over a bit longer before responding and then said: 'It depends: two and two can be four, but it can also be twenty two!' This means that she is good at analyzing situations and exploring different alternatives, but she may have difficulty in making a decision. Which of the three would you prefer?"

The CEO looked at the pictures of the three candidates and replied: "I want the one with the big boobs!"

This response, of course, is the nightmare of Human Resources professionals, who do a serious job out of selecting candidates, but often find that line managers end up making their final hiring decisions based on the wrong criteria, and ignoring all the hard work done by the HR staff involved. Yet, this often happens in real life, and if you are in HR, you need to be prepared to handle such situations. The final hiring decision should always be made by the line manager; the role of HR should be to help managers make that decision, coaching them to use technically sound criteria, free of any kind of prejudice or discrimination.

19. Sister Math and Sister Logic

This story illustrates the important difference between Mathematics and Logic, two disciplines that are often used in the decision making process promoted in Business Schools and employed in large corporations.

Sister Math and Sister Logic were two catholic nuns who were so named for their dedication to these two disciplines. Every evening they would also teach at the village Night School, returning afterwards to their convent on a hill just outside the town.

One evening, as they left the school together, Sister Math look over her shoulder and whispered: "Sister Logic, I think that man in a raincoat is following us..."

"Let's walk faster. If he walks faster too, we will have an indication that he might indeed be following us," replied Sister Logic.

"I calculated that he was about 20 meters behind us," said Sister Math. "After we hurried our steps, I just calculated that he is still 20 meters behind us."

"Let's cross the street and walk on the opposite sidewalk, and see if he does the same thing," suggested Sister Logic.

"He crossed the street and he is gaining on us... He is just 15 meters behind us!" said Sister Math.

"We are almost outside of town, on the road up to the convent. Can we reach the convent before he catches up with us? Sister Logic asked.

"At the rate he is walking, I calculated that he will catch up with us 300 meters before we reach the convent!" said Sister Math.

"Let's run for it!" whispered Sister Logic anxiously.

As they started running, it was clear that Sister Math was a much faster runner than Sister Logic. Soon she was further ahead and Sister Logic was falling behind. As Sister Math looked back, she saw that the man caught up with Sister Logic. Sister Math ran even faster, thinking "I have to get to the convent and get help!"

When she finally got to the convent, she was out of breath. The other nuns and the Mother Superior gathered around her and offered some water. It took some time before she could recover and recount her woeful tale. As the sisters debated what to do, call the police or go down to the village immediately, they saw someone running up the road towards the convent. It was Sister Logic!

When she arrived she was also out of breath and needed some water and some more time to recover. The whole convent was now standing eagerly around her, asking what had happened.

"Well," she said, gasping for air. "The man reached me and pushed me against a wall..."

"And then what happened, my child?" asked the Mother Superior.

"He ordered me to raise my robes above my waist."

"Oohh!" exclaimed the nuns around her. "And then?"

"Then he lowered his pants below his knees."

"Oohh!" the nuns exclaimed again. "And then?"

"The logical thing happened..." said Sister Logic with a wry smile on her lips. "A nun with her robes raised above her waist can run much faster than a man with his pants around his ankles!"

Many managers pay too much attention to numbers (and Math), while not giving enough consideration to whether or not the numbers actually make sense (Logic). The role of managers is not to check whether the numbers add up (operational staff should be checking that); the role of managers is to analyze the information conveyed by the figures, understand their logic, and to make decisions based on that.

To do that, they sometimes also use their intuition, which is linked unconsciously to Logic and not simply to numbers and Math. Overall, Logic has greater impact on business decisions than figures ever will, regardless of what they may tell you at an MBA course.

20. Lawyer Looking for a Parking Spot

Sometimes decisions have to be made very quickly, especially when you are an unscrupulous lawyer.

A lawyer was driving for a court hearing but got stuck in traffic and was risking to be late. He drove to the court building but could not find a place to park. He started driving around the block, looking for a parking space. All spaces were occupied and the clock was ticking...

He closed his eyes for a second and made a quick prayer: "Oh Lord, please, please, help me find a parking space! If you get me a spot, I promise I'll go to church every Sunday for a whole year!"

When he opened his eyes, he saw a free parking space just in front of him. "Never mind, Lord! I just found a space!"

This illustrates how some people may behave unethically whenever there is an opportunity to avoid fulfilling their side of a bargain, even when the other party is the Almighty!

In my experience, senior managers often ask their staff "is this legal?" before deciding on a proposed course of action. Indeed, they often enlist the help of lawyers to provide a professional opinion. In addition to that, managers should ask themselves "is this right?" The law often leaves open loopholes that allow companies to do certain things without going against written regulations. However, from an ethical perspective, you need to ask yourself if what is about to be done is something that is beyond reproach, regardless of legal stipulations.

21. One Man, Three Whiskies

A man came into a bar and ordered three whiskies, straight, no ice.

"Would you like to have a triple?" asked the bartender. He had just started working at this bar, it was his first day.

"No," said the man. "Please pour me three whiskies, one in each glass.

The bartender did as he was asked. The man started drinking, leisurely, and the bartender stepped aside to do some chores, clean glasses, tend to other clients.

The next day, at about the same time in the evening, the man returned and asked again for three whiskies. This time the bartender asked no questions, he simply poured the three whiskies in three glasses.

After a while the bartender couldn't resist his curiosity any longer, so he asked the man: "Sir, please excuse my curiosity, but why do you come here each day and ask for three shots in three different glasses?"

The man replied: "No need to excuse yourself, I guess it does look kind of odd to a bystander. The thing is, I had three buddies and we would always come here every day after work. For years we did that, every day from Monday to Friday. But now my buddies have both passed away... I like coming down here and having a whisky myself, and one for each of them, as a kind of tribute to our friendship."

"That's a beautiful story!" remarked the bartender. And he stepped to one side, leaving the man to his memories.

After a couple of weeks of the same daily routine, one day the man comes in and asks: "Bartender, two whiskies please."

The bartender pours him the two whiskies in two glasses, and once again cannot resist his curiosity: "Pardon me for asking, but why are you having only two whiskies? What happened?"

The man responds: "I just did a medical check-up and the doctor told me I have some health problems, so I decided to quit drinking!"

When you decide to do something, make sure that you really mean it and that you are not just trying to fool anyone, especially yourself!

22. Reducing a Big Issue in Size

Sometimes managers are faced with big, complex issue about which they must decide, and the issue seems too big to handle. When advising executives on such situations, I sometimes tell them the following story, as a way to release the tension, before getting into the issue at hand, in a serious fashion.

I typically say: "It would be great if you could handle this issue in the same way that the Slobonian did when he went to Africa hunting for elephants…"

And then I tell them the story.

A Slobonian was about to go out on a Safari in Africa hunting for elephants. He went into a shop to buy an elephant gun and explained to the shopkeeper why he needed it.

The man behind the counter had a sense of humor, so he replied: "Well, actually, to hunt elephants you don't need a gun at all!"

"I don't need a gun?" asked the amazed Slobonian.

"Not at all. All you need is a pair of binoculars, an empty matchbox, and a pair of tweezers."

The Slobonian was increasingly puzzled. "How am I going to hunt an elephant with that?"

"Simple," replied the shopkeeper. "Take the items with you. When you're out in Africa and you spot an elephant, go after it until you are standing right next to it, very close. Then take the binoculars and reverse them, looking at the elephant from the lens side of the binoculars: the elephant will seem very small. Then, just take the pair of tweezers and put the tiny elephant into the matchbox!"

In real life this does not apply to real issues; but getting someone to laugh about their predicament can be helpful to ease anxiety and clear the mind, improving their chances of tackling the large problem more effectively. Perhaps it is just a matter of perspective; when you are able to look at a problem from a distant point of view, you are better able to see it as something solvable and not as something threatening. This may help you find a solution to your predicament.

PART III – ORGANIZATIONAL CULTURE

23. The Bamboo Church

Thousands of years ago, somewhere in China, there were two villages facing each other on opposite sides of a river. On a certain year, the people in one village decided that they should build a temple. They gathered all the villagers, agreed on the design and started to build a medium-sized structure that could hold all the villagers in prayer, made of bamboo, which was plentiful along the river banks.

The villagers on the other side of the river saw what was going on and decided that they should also build a place of worship. However, the elders of their village thought it over and decided that their temple should be made of stones and not of bamboo. They concluded that it would take longer to build, but the finished building would last longer and would resist the strong winds and the rainstorms that often passed through that area.

The bamboo church on the first village was ready within two months; meanwhile, the stone church was barely in its foundation.

When the winter storms struck, part of the bamboo church was torn down. The villagers had to spend a week to rebuild it. The stone church was not finished until three years had passed. There was a big ceremony with offerings to the gods to declare it officially open for services.

As time went by, the stone church resisted the winds and the rain pretty well; the bamboo church had to be repaired after every storm.

After a few years went by, a strange thing was observed: the people in the second village went less and less to the church services. They took the church for granted and on each week fewer people came to it, until finally it was just the priest there with one or two villagers. The people felt that the church belonged to the priest, and the little maintenance that was required, could easily be carried out by him.

The people of the first village continued in high attendance to their church year after year. They were constantly repairing and rebuilding the church and they knew that if they did not remain committed to doing this, the church would disappear. The people felt *that the church belonged to the village and it was up to them to keep it fit and functioning.*

This story illustrates the need for involvement and participation in order to get engagement and maintain a sense of belonging, of identity, and a strong corporate culture. People need to feel that they own the culture and that they belong to it; that they are, ultimately, the culture.

If people have the feeling that the culture is just an abstract construct that is owned by "the corporation" (whatever that means) or by the Chief Executive Priest (I mean, Officer), then they will become detached and the culture will be meaningless, just a poster on a wall.

Participation is key in matters of organizational culture; otherwise, it becomes a meaningless corporate exercise designed for senior managers to fool themselves.

24. The Family with a Cow

About a thousand years ago, in medieval Europe, there lived a family in a tiny farm that had just one cow, next to a river. The family was just the farmer, his wife, a son and a daughter. They lived a very modest life, in a small house with a single room that served as kitchen, dining room and bedroom for all four, growing their own food, and selling the milk that the cow provided. This gave them barely enough revenue to pay the king's tax and survive.

One evening a traveler knocked on their door and asked for shelter. They were very kind and took him in, sharing the little that they had to eat for supper, and offering him some space to lie down and sleep in front of the fireplace. They spoke candidly to him about the simple life that they led, and of how fortunate they were to have the cow as a source of revenue.

That night, while everyone was asleep, the traveler went outside, took the cow by tow and pushed it off a cliff. The next morning, the family woke up and discovered that both the traveler and the cow had disappeared.

They cried together at their misfortune; apparently the traveler had stolen the cow. Now their source of revenue was gone and they would not have enough money to pay their taxes to the king! They risked losing the farm, the only thing they had... What would they do?

Five years went by, and one day the traveler returned to the little farm. At first, he did not recognize the place: the house was bigger than he remembered, and there was now a barn behind the house. But he recognized the river and the rest of the landscape, so he concluded that this was, indeed, the same place.

He knocked on the door; the mother opened it and immediately recognized him. Instead of expressing anger, she welcomed him inside and called out to her husband and her children, who by now were almost young adults. They all greeted the traveler cheerfully.

"I see some things have changed around here..." commented the traveler.

"Indeed they have," responded the farmer. "When we had to face our new reality without the cow, we were forced to come up with alternatives: my wife started to sell her services as a seamstress; our boy began fishing at the river and we sold the fish that were in excess of our own needs; our daughter helped me to plant more vegetables and fruit that we could sell at the town market. Soon we began to prosper; now we could afford to have a barn to store our produce, we bought another cow, an ox and a cart to take our goods to the market, we enlarged the house... Now we have separate bedrooms!"

He went on: "At first we were distraught and cursed the day you came to our home; but now we realized that it was actually a blessing. Taking the cow away made us become less complacent; we were able to do much more and now we have more comfort, while at the same time we are producing more and helping others. So we are thankful for what you've done."

"I'm glad to hear," responded the traveler. "In all truth, I'm a traveling consultant with McKingsey & Partners; you will be getting our invoice soon for our intervention in your situation!"

Many companies have "cash-cows", standard products or services that bring them steady revenue and make them not only comfortable, but also complacent as an organization. A good exercise is to think about what would happen to the company if suddenly that "cash-cow" was gone (made obsolete by competitors, for instance)...

Can the organization reinvent itself? Does it have untapped creative resources that might be used to generate new products and services? Is the company fulfilling all of its potential? What could be done to plan for positive change, rather than be surprised by negative change coming from an unexpected source (such as an aggressive competitor or a hostile take-over)? Depending on a single "cash-cow" can be very risky; companies need to mitigate risk by developing alternative sources of revenue.

Food for thought.

25. The Old Lady at the Doctor

A very old lady came to a doctor and told him: "I haven't had any health problems in years, despite my getting on the years. However, in the past twelve months I've had a nagging issue that is a little embarrassing... At first I thought it would go away by itself, but the months went by and it continued. I tried changing my diet, drinking different kinds of teas, but nothing worked. That's when I decided to come to you."

"Don't worry," said the doctor, "nothing is embarrassing to a doctor. Just tell me what your problem is."

"It's gasses," she said, blushing a bit. "I know this can happen with age. I'm constantly feeling a bit of pain in my belly, and to relieve it I must pass gasses... Thank heavens that they are always noiseless, and they also don't smell bad, so nobody around me notices anything. But it is annoying to me, I feel this constant discomfort in my belly."

"Take these pills two times a day and come back in a week; I want to check your progress." He gave her a prescription and she left.

A week later she was back, but she seemed even more annoyed than she was on her first consultation.

"Doctor," she complained, "these pills you gave me are awful! They did not relieve my gasses at all. And what is worse, now my gasses smell terrible! I can't stand them! I'm worse off than I was when I got here!"

Doctor wrote her another prescription and explained: "the pills I gave you had the purpose of clearing up your nose and give you back your sense of smell, which you clearly had lost. The medicine I am giving you today will give you back your sense of hearing; you are almost completely deaf. Come back in another week for me to see if this is working, and then we will treat your problem with gasses!"

The problem with diagnosing organizational culture is that, often, top management think that they know what the company's problem is, but it turns out that they are blind to what the real problem actually is. That is why it is always good to get an external consultant to look at your culture, with an objective and unbiased perspective. Such a professional may tell you to look at some aspects that are more important than what you initially thought was the issue.

Diagnostics is where culture change begins: you first need to agree on the problems, before you can try to agree on solutions. And as Edgar Schein points out (see "References" at the end of this book): organizational culture issues need to focus on solving a concrete problem, otherwise they are just an academic exercise. Getting a good diagnostic, therefore, is a pre-condition to tackle organization culture.

But it is just the beginning of a long and complex process.

26. A Spoon and a Cord Tied to Your Zipper

Trying to change a culture in a certain direction, according to the intentions of senior management is often a difficult endeavor, fraught with obstacles and unseen problems. One of these is that people frequently give their own interpretations to what senior management is trying to do. This may result in behaviors quite different from what the original intention of management was.

A new manager was appointed to a rather traditional restaurant in London. As he surveyed the situation of the place during his first week on the job, he was shocked to find that the waiters and the kitchen staff displayed several disturbing habits that were very unhygienic.

For instance, the kitchen staff often dipped their index finger into a plate of soup and sucked on it, just before it was going to be taken to the client's table, to check for temperature and whether the soup had the right amount of salt. The manager found this absolutely disgusting and totally unacceptable.

He gathered all staff and ordered them to each have a spoon hanging by a thread fastened to their belts. Whenever they needed to taste the soup, they were to use their personal spoon and clean it afterwards.

The manager also noticed that kitchen staff took frequent breaks to go to the men's room. He did not want them handling their trousers' zippers with their hands and returning immediately to the kitchen. He ordered all staff, as of the next day, to attach a slender chain to their zippers, with the other end fastened around their wrists. This would allow the men to open and close their zippers without touching them, just by using swift movements of their arms.

He urged staff to wash their hands before leaving the rest rooms, and also to never touch their penises while urinating.

The next day, as the staff tried earnestly to follow the new instructions, two kitchen assistants met at the men's room. One of them asks to the other, by the urinal:

"Hey, this is totally awkward... How am I supposed to get my

penis back in my pants if I can't touch it?"
The other replies: "I don't know about the others, but I just use my spoon!"

People are practical, above all, and they will try to find solutions that are easiest to implement as they go about handling their daily tasks. When management tries to set standards of behavior, they need to look carefully at how the standards will affect the simple things that people need to do to get their job done.

What looks good on paper at a Corporate Board meeting may prove to be unfeasible in practice on the shop floor. It is always good to enlist the advice of people directly involved with the operational aspects of execution, and putting changes through the test of pilot projects, independently evaluated before implementing full-scale modifications in procedures. This not only improves the quality of the final solution; it also increases staff engagement in implementing the changes.

27. Two Statisticians Hunting Deer

Beware diagnostic reports of organizational culture making heavy use of numbers and statistics. Figures need to be interpreted very carefully. Some people have cautioned against using statistical reports at face value, saying that in this world there are lies, damn lies and statistics; others have said that statistics is like a bikini: it shows everything but what is essential.

This story illustrates the need to always interpret statistical reports with a very critical and skeptical attitude, and to challenge statements made by statisticians.

Two statistics specialists were out in the woods together hunting deer. Suddenly, they spot a stag quietly grazing several yards away. They both take careful aim and shoot at the same time.

The first guy's shot was off to the right and just missed the deer; the second guy's shot was off to the left and missed the target too.

They look at each other and shout: "We got him!"

The "average" individual in any population is someone that does not actually exist. "Average" is an abstract construct, derived from mathematical calculations about the population as a group, but it does not correspond to any of the actual members of that group.

So when you talk about "the average client" or "the average staff member" of your organization, do bear in mind that you will never actually meet such a person; this person does not exist. Any statements made about "the average individual" need to be taken with more than just a grain of salt.

28. The Good Rooster

A young American money desk trader took his first hugely overblown bonus and went to celebrate by traveling to Mexico for the first time. He wanted to experience "the real Mexico", so after checking in at his exclusive six-star resort, he went to check out the nearby village, mingling with the locals.

He came upon a rooster fighting ring, were many men were gathered drinking tequila, cheering and placing big bets on the roosters who fought in a small, improvised arena.

Always keen to place a bet on any kind of sports event, the trader elbowed his way to the front string of people around the ring and started a conversation with one of the locals.

"Hey, I want to place a bet in one of these roosters that are going to fight next. How about this one?" he asked, pointing to a white rooster with a bright red comb strutting about proudly.

"That rooster is good", remarked the Mexican, with an accent thicker than an enchilada.

The other rooster in the arena was smaller, scrawny and dark grey, looking like he had just walked into the arena by mistake. The gringo bet $500 on the white rooster.

The fight lasted less than a minute. As soon as it started, the dark grey rooster jumped on the other and beat the shit out of him. They had to stop the fight before the white rooster got killed.

"Hey!" complained the gringo to the guy next to him. "I just lost $500 bucks in one minute! I thought you said the white rooster was good!"

"Señor," replied the Mexican in his slow drawl, "the white rooster is good. The grey rooster is bad, he is really mean..."

When you join a new organization and you are trying to learn what the culture is like, or rather, simply trying to figure out how things are done around here, be careful about how you interpret the answers to your questions.

You may be asking pretty simple and straightforward questions; however, the answers you get back will necessarily be tinted by the local culture. When you don't know that culture, you may not get the true meaning of what is being said to you, with all its nuances and connotations.

PART IV – HIERARCHY

29. The Maestro

The concept of Power Distance, a term coined by Geert Hofstede and widely used when referring to hierarchical cultures, is the most frequently identified problem when managing across cultures. Managers brought up in a culture of low Power Distance, also referred to as egalitarian cultures, find it difficult to understand and operate as effectively when assigned to work in a hierarchical cultural environment (it's equally difficult for managers from a hierarchical culture to be as effective in an egalitarian one).

The story below helps to illustrate how hierarchical cultures work, and so do the other stories in this "Part 4" of the book.

An orchestra was rehearsing during their twice weekly practice session, when the maestro suddenly interrupted the symphony they were playing, very annoyed.

"Stop, stop, stop!" he shouted. After pausing a bit for suspense, he remarked: "The third violin on the second string row is playing in F major, when this part should be in F minor!" A deep silence fell on the whole room. You might be able to hear a needle drop on the floor.

One of the violinists stood up hesitantly in the middle of the musicians and said: "Excuse me, Sir, but the third violin on the second string row did not come for the rehearsal today, he is absent…"

"Well, when he comes, tell him!" said the irritated maestro.

The boss is always right; even when the boss is wrong, he is right. Live with it!

This might be true everywhere, but even more so in high Power Distance cultures.

30. When You Look Up

They say that hierarchical organizations are like a bunch of monkeys, distributed throughout the branches of a tree at different levels. When you are on the top branches and you look down, all you see is smiling faces looking up at you.

When you are in the bottom branches looking up, all you see is a bunch of assholes!

In a hierarchical culture, people at the top of the structure are frequently pampered and praised by the people below. (See also my books "Take Off Your Glasses" and "Crossing Cultures.") This is because people in the lower part of the hierarchy tend to attribute a huge amount of power to the positions on top, regardless of how their occupants actually behave in practice. People at the bottom are afraid of all that power, whether it is real or imagined, whether it is exercised or not. The possibility of it being exercised is more frightening than what actually happens.

Because of this fear, mistakes and bad news are frequently hidden from senior managers. People are afraid of their reaction, they think that the boss will be angry and will punish them severely. Therefore, whenever the boss looks down upon them, their default attitude is to smile and say that "all is well".

At the same time that this is their overt behavior, often times they criticize their bosses behind their backs (never to the boss' face, of course; they are too afraid to confront the boss). People at the bottom of the hierarchy tend to get little information from above; usually the managers have access to information that is centralized, concentrated at the top, and not available to the lower levels of the corporate pyramid.

This means that, frequently, top managers make decisions that seem incomprehensible to the people below. Senior managers also seldom explain their decisions, contributing to an image of "those guys up there do not know what they are doing! We have to do as we are told in order to avoid punishment, but we are the ones who really know what the important issues are, the guys on top are just assholes who don't have a clue about what it's like to do our job on the shop floor!"

Perception, of course, is reality. Top management may be making all the right decisions, based on the information available only to them; but when they don't bother to explain these decisions, to the people at the bottom it appears that they don't know what they're doing.

31. When You Make a Huge Blunder

When you make a blunder, you get punished or you may even get fired. But when you make a huge blunder, you get promoted and transferred to Head Office!

In hierarchical organizations there is often a sort of collegial conspiracy among the senior management members to protect each other, consciously or unconsciously.

When somebody makes a mistake in a clerical position lower down in the structure, often the simple solution is to fire that person without much hesitation.

When a mistake is made among the managers of a region or country, (the higher the position, the bigger the potential impact of the mistake) typically there is a tendency to cover up or minimize the issue, because it would be rather embarrassing to admit that someone at such a high position is also liable for such big mistakes. Often there is a manoeuver designed to avoid embarrassment, and that is to kick the culprit upstairs, rather than to kick him out. If that someone is actually transferred abroad, to the global company's Headquarters, for instance, most people are happy… except eventually the staff workers who can see through the manoeuver and gossip about it at the water cooler. Hence the comment made above, which is a real-life comment often made in Latin America about certain Country Management Team members who were not highly regarded locally, but who got promoted to positions in the US or in Europe in spite of their local reputation of poor effectiveness.

Another way of expressing their disapproval ironically is through the expression "for the same mistakes, small fish get punished, big fish get promoted!"

32. Three Parrots

A man walks into a pet shop and asks to buy a parrot to keep him company as a pet. The shop owner motions him to where he keeps the birds and shows him three nice specimens in the same cage.

"This first one looks nice," says the man. "How much do you want for it?"

"This one will be $5,000," replies the shopkeeper.

"Wow!" exclaims the man. "I had no idea that a parrot could be so expensive... Can he talk?"

"Of course he can talk," says the shopkeeper. "This is a very special parrot. Not only can he talk, but if you leave him watching the 7 o'clock news, he will later repeat to you all the news he has heard. It's like having a recorder without the need for batteries!"

"Yes, that is very impressive," agrees the client. "But it's actually a bit above my budget. How about this second parrot? How much is this one?"

"This one is $10,000," replies de shopkeeper.

"You're kidding me!" says the customer.

"No I'm not. This is an extremely special parrot. He can talk, and if you leave him watching the 7 o'clock news, not only will he repeat the broadcast to you, word by word, he will also add his own political and economics commentaries!"

"Impressive, no doubt," says the man, "but it's far too expensive for me. How about this third parrot?"

"That one is $20,000" says the shopkeeper.

"Unbelievable!" exclaims the man. "And what does he do? Does he speak several languages, or what?"

"Actually, he doesn't do anything much," explains the shopkeeper. "He doesn't speak a lot, he just sits around and does nothing. But the other two call him 'Boss', so he must be worth much more!"

This story illustrates the power of hierarchy in determining pay structures and compensation in general. Most hierarchical organizations pay according to position and not according to performance, even if they declare the opposite. It also illustrates the point that often managers don't seem to be doing very much... their role is to supervise and coach people who actually execute tasks, and that is perceived as not being real "work".

Managing is not, indeed, about "doing" things; rather, it is about analyzing, deciding and mobilizing.

Analyzing means considering situations, problems to solve, weighing different courses of action. In order to do that, managers need to have the so-called "helicopter capacity": the ability to rise above a problem, take a different perspective and look at things from a broader point of view. This allows them to see things more clearly, perceiving the broader implications of issues and the wide-ranging impact of what could be done.

Deciding on a course of action means making decisions that they can live with, considering the emotional consequences of their decisions. Looking at logic and figures is necessary, but above that is the issue of coping with the emotional consequences of choosing something over a different thing. Even if the numbers "tell" you to do something for the good of the company, will you able to do that if it means hurting certain people that are dear to you? Will you do something that goes against your personal values? Many managers get "paralysis by analysis" when they are unable to cope with these emotional consequences. This is much more difficult than it seems.

Finally, managers need to be capable of mobilizing their teams and their companies to support and carry out their decisions, to execute strategy effectively. A manager without followers is not leading an army, he/she is just taking a walk in the woods (by himself or herself).

All this may not seem like "work" to some people; but it is more important, more difficult and more valuable, which is why managers earn more than those who just "do work!"

PART V – MANAGING ACROSS CULTURES

33. The Game of Cachanga

A gringo walks into a seedy bar in a remote village in Mexico. He orders a tequila at the bar and notices that a group of people are huddled around a card table where some locals are playing cards. Always interested in a competition, the gringo walks over to take a closer look.

They are, indeed, playing cards, but it doesn't look like poker. It doesn't look like anything like he's ever seen before. The players hold many cards in their hands and place heavy bets.

A big fat guy on the far side of the table seems to be winning, he has a lot of chips and money bills in front of him. He looks like he's a bandit come straight out of a Western movie: unshaven, big cigar at the corner of his mouth, two ammunition belts crossing over his chest, sombrero hanging over his back held by a leather strap on his neck.

The big Mexican sees the gringo by the table and shouts:

"Hey gringo! You no watch! You play!" He motions the American to sit down on an empty chair in front of him.

"But I don't know how to play..."

"Shut up! Sit down! Play!"

Everybody in the bar gives the gringo a nasty look. He decides to go along and see if he can figure out the rules as they play a few rounds. It can't be that hard.

The big guy deals the cards, nine to each player, and lays the remainder of the deck at the center of the table. He takes one card from the top of the mound, and lays off another card, face up on the table.

"Hmm," the gringo thinks, "maybe this is a little bit like canasta?"

Other players follow similar moves. He picks a card and looks at what he has on his hand. He can't figure out what kind of sets is he supposed to make: sequences? Trios?

Suddenly the big Mexican lays all his cards face up on the table and shouts "Cachanga!". All players fold, and the big guy collects all bets dragging the money and chips to his side of the table.

The gringo didn't have time to see what kind of set or sequence were on the guy's cards, as they were also quickly collected.

The big guy is shuffling the deck. The gringo decides he will have to pay more attention this time.

The game goes on like before. Suddenly, the big Mexican shouts "Cachanga!" again and puts his cards on the table. He quickly collects the bets and the cards like before, so quickly that the gringo still does not know what is happening.

As they go for a third round, the gringo decides to try something. He suddenly yells "Cachanga!" and lays all his cards face up in front of him.

The big guy immediately lays his own cards on the table and shouts "Cachanga Real!"

When working in a new culture and learning "how things are done here," be aware that the locals have more room to manoeuver than you do. You may think that you have figured out "the rules of the game..." but since they made the rules, they can also change them, or make them up as they go along, or simply reveal a deeper layer of the rules that at first was not apparent.

The latter is more often the case. Culture is complex and does indeed have more layers than you may initially think. Tread carefully, and have a local friend by your side, to help you find your way.

34. The Armadillo

An American lawyer is driving through a side-road in Mexico, when he sees something in the middle of the road looking like a large stone; he decides to stop and see what it is.

Upon close inspection, he realizes that it's an armadillo, rolled up like a ball to protect itself. "Why is this guy lying here in the middle of the road," he thinks to himself. "He might get run over by a careless driver. Hmm, maybe he's hurt. I'd better take him with me to the next town and see if I find someone to look after him."

He puts the beast in the trunk and drives on. As soon as he joins the highway, he runs into a road block set up by the Highway Patrol. A policeman steps up to his window, asks him for documentation and tells him to open the trunk for inspection.

As soon as the patrolman sees the Armadillo, he turns to the lawyer: "Whoa! Mister, you are in trouble! This is a protected species; you cannot take it with you! If I tell the Environmental Protection Agency about this, you will be arrested... This is a serious crime!"

"What? You've got it all wrong. This armadillo is my pet! I've had him since he was a baby. I take him with me everywhere. He even comes to me when I whistle."

"You are pulling my leg, Señor... I never heard of training an armadillo..."

"Here, I'll prove it to you." He takes the armadillo and puts it on the ground. As soon as the animal is on the pavement, it runs towards the side of the road and disappears in the bushes.

"OK," says the policeman. "Now you whistle and let's see if the armadillo comes back to you."

"Armadillo? What armadillo?"

Lawyers learn how to think fast and turn on a dime to change their arguments, when necessary. This may come in handy when dealing with unexpected situations abroad. And in these cross-culture stories, the visitor to a country is not always the fall guy...

35. Western Questions to a Chinese Professor

Jane Smith was an American doctor specialized in neurology. She has dedicated herself to treating pain symptoms and in the previous three years had researched Chinese acupuncture as an alternative approach to treating pain.

During her research Dr. Smith came across the name of a Chinese scholar, Professor Chen Wang, from the University of Beijing, who was often referred to as the leading Chinese authority in acupuncture. However, none of his books on the subject had ever been translated from the original Mandarin language he wrote them on. Although she found that Dr. Wang was often mentioned in English-language medical articles, she was unable to find any translation of his original writings

Smith was very happy to discover, through a colleague from the University of Singapore, that Professor Wang would soon be teaching a special three-day intensive course in English. It would be offered in Singapore, where he was a visiting professor. The course was aimed at medical students and doctors based in Singapore, but open to outsiders as well. With the help of the same colleague, she was able to secure a spot as a pupil among the group.

She made her travel arrangements hastily, managed to obtain a one-week leave of absence at the hospital she was working at in Boston, and flew to Singapore arriving there one day before the program began.

She was fairly aware of the fact that there would be culture differences in Singapore, although her friends in the States that had previously been there as tourists had assured her that Singapore was quite international and cosmopolitan, and she would be fine as long as she respected the severe regulations about littering and smoking.

She was very excited as she sat through the first day of the course, taking notes of every word uttered by the professor, but at the end of that day she knew that something was terribly wrong and she called a friend in the Netherlands who was a consultant on culture issues, for help.

"I don't know what's going on, but I must be doing something wrong", she said on the phone. "I can see that the professor became increasingly irritated with me as the day went on. As the morning session ended, I tried to approach him to tell him how much I was enjoying the course, but he quickly hurried to the cafeteria when he saw me approaching him in the classroom. At the cafeteria I was unable to sit with him, as he was surrounded by other students. He left the dining room in a hurry and went into the teacher's lounge, which is off-limits to course students. When he came back to the classroom he began lecturing immediately and I didn't have a chance to speak to him. As the afternoon went on, he ignored my questions, although he would answer the questions posed by other Chinese students."

"Did you try to ask him about this in the afternoon?" inquired the consultant.

"He was definitely avoiding me", Jane replied. "During the break, he fled to the men's room and only came out to resume his lecturing. At the end of the day he apologized and left in a hurry, mentioning another appointment. Yet I could see him chatting leisurely with other students later in front of the main entrance."

"Did you ask him any questions during the lecture?" asked the consultant.

"Yes, of course!" said Jane. "I wanted to demonstrate my interest in the subject! But I was careful to be very polite, so I always began with: 'Excuse me, professor, may I ask you a question?' and then I formulated my question. I could see that the other students were also getting annoyed with me, but they sometimes also asked questions."

"What kind of questions did you ask?"

Jane reflected a bit before responding. "They were mostly questions like 'Why is it that when you insert a needle in the lower ear lobe that will have an effect on the patient's pancreas?', you know, things like that. I could see that the professor was uncomfortable and sometimes he just ignored my question and answered someone else's question instead. Do you think it was because I am a woman?"

"Probably not. What kind of questions did the other pupils ask?"

Jane stopped again to think before replying: "I guess they were more about 'how do you position the needle, or how do you determine the exact point of entry on the skin', questions like that."

"That's probably the reason he was annoyed," said the consultant. He is open to "how" questions, more than to "why".

Many Asian cultures and especially the Chinese are more focused on "how" rather than "why" issues.

Western questions are more analytical, inquiring the "why", trying to break down a situation into different parts, establishing relations of cause and effect among these parts, in order to later be able to reproduce certain parts and obtain similar outcomes. The emphasis is on cause and effect, in order to perform planned change (or even disruptive change) in other situations.

In the Chinese culture it is more important to accept the world as it is and understand **how** things work. That way, in another situation, you can use what is already there in order to obtain certain effects. The difference lies in not focusing so much on the analysis of separate parts, but rather on understanding the whole as presented in each situation. Reality is what it is; the better you understand how things work, the better you will be able to get what you want in a situation, with minimal disruptive impact.

The professor was embarrassed and annoyed because, basically, he does not know **why** acupuncture works the way it does. One of the reasons he does not know that, is that he never focused on the "why." He must have spent half of his life learning the "how", and that is what made him famous. That is also what he is trying to teach to others: **how** to do it.

To use a more typically American analogy: imagine that you are a young baseball player trying to learn from a great pitcher how to throw a curve ball. The experienced pro can probably teach you how to do it and help you practice until you get it right; but if you ask him **why** the ball travels on a curved path if thrown in a certain way, he might not be able to explain this to you.

In North-Western cultures people believe that science should always be about understanding the "why" (cause and effect) and measuring results quantitatively. They think that this is a universal concept of what may be considered "science." However, in Eastern and Southern cultures there is more of an overlap between art and science; the latter may encompass also some areas of knowledge that are not quantifiable or that do not include understanding the "why", but focusing on the "how." The notion of what is "science," therefore, is not really universal. Rather, it is influenced by culture.

36. Reception in Peru

A Dutch businessman is on his first trip to Peru and he attends a reception at the Dutch Embassy in Lima. He arrives promptly at 7pm, the time stated on the written invitation he received, and notices that he is the first guest to arrive. He stands by himself in a big ballroom and takes a glass of the "pisco sauer" that is offered to him by a waiter. It tastes surprisingly good and he soon has another one, still waiting for the other guests.

At around 7:30 a few other people begin to arrive, most of them foreigners living in Peru. The Dutchman had only had a "broodje" to eat for lunch at 12:00 pm, and he was used to having his supper at 6:00; by now he was starving, but dinner was nowhere in sight. At least there was plenty of "pisco sauer" going around to distract him from his hunger.

By 8:30 most guests had arrived and the Dutchman was completely drunk. He lost count of how many drinks he had, but they were all delicious, he was feeling just fine...

An official-looking gentleman at the far end of the room said something in Spanish and music started to play loudly. The Dutchman thought: "great, the ball begins!" Full of initiative, he grabbed an old lady standing next to him by the waist and started waltzing around the floor.

She looked a bit startled with his bold move, so he chatted to break the ice: "I just arrived today to your beautiful country, tell me some tips about your culture!"

"I will tell you three things, Sir: first, never have more than one "pisco" on an empty stomach; second, this is not a waltz, it's the national anthem; and third, I'm not a lady, I'm the archbishop of Lima!"

When visiting a foreign country, be especially cautious with the local liquors... You probably don't realize how strong they really are, no matter how smooth they taste!

And when joining a party that includes music and dancing, make sure that you really know what is expected regarding the music and what kind of dancing (if any), before you take to the floor and make a fool of yourself...

This applies, of course, also to other situations. The notions of "when in Rome, do as the Romans do", or trying to "dance according to the music" fail to emphasize that, to a foreigner, things appear to have a certain meaning that does not necessarily coincide with the meaning intended by the locals.

Context is codified. Situations always have certain connotations that are interpreted by the locals in a certain way, and are interpreted by foreigners in a different way, consistent with their respective cultures. You should first check with a local whether your interpretation of the context is appropriate, before taking the leap to act in a way that might make sense in your home culture, but might be totally silly to the eyes of everyone else locally.

37. The Little German Boy Who Did Not Speak

There once was a little German boy who was four years old and had not yet said a single word. His parents were worried and took him to a doctor.

The doctor examined the boy and found nothing wrong. He said: "some children learn to speak a little later than others. Just be patient."

When the boy was five years old, still he did not speak. So the parents took him to a specialist. The specialist did all kinds of tests and declared: "there is nothing wrong with the boy. Just give him some more time."

When he turned six years of age he still did not speak... The parents took him to Berlin, to the best clinic in Germany. They ran all kinds of tests, even a computer scan. Still, they could not find anything wrong with the boy.

The three of them returned home. The parents were disappointed, because they could not find out what was wrong. As they sat down to dinner, the boy took a spoonful of his soup and said "the soup is cold."

The father almost had a heart attack! He shouted, "my God, you can speak! Why haven't you ever said a word?!"

The boy responded: "Up until now, everything was in order..."

German culture is all about order, discipline, structure and procedures. If careful planning is done, and everyone fulfills their role in executing plans according to clear specifications, then everything should work "like a well-oiled machine."

Germans believe that problems arise when people are not disciplined, when they do not take their responsibilities seriously, when they do not comply with what is expected of them.

38. Trapped in an Earthquake

A strong earthquake in a South American village left everything destroyed, most buildings reduced to piles of rubble. Rescue teams were quickly formed and help came from all over the world, using sophisticated equipment and also rescue dogs trained to sniff if there were survivors trapped beneath the rubble.

As different teams were searching the debris, a team member shouted to the others: "Over here, my dog has found someone!"

They were standing on a pile of bricks and mortar that once had been a small tourist hotel. They could hear a German tourist trapped beneath the rubble. They could not see him, but they could definitely hear him.

"We can hear you, Sir! Are you hurt?"

"Ach!" shouted the German. "I have scratches und bruises, but I'm OK. There are stones and wooden beams on top of me, so I can't move, but I think I haven't broken any bones."

"Don't worry, Sir! We'll get you out! We have to start removing the rubble so that we can free you!"

"OK," shouted the German. "I'm in room 27!"

Germans will always try to hold on to patterns and structures, even when some people would think that everything has fallen apart. The German ethos is to try to find structure even amidst chaos.

39. Four People on a Train

Four passengers are sharing the same cabin on a train: a pretty young lady, an elderly woman, an Argentinian man and a Brazilian man. They ride for a while, entertained by their own thoughts, without exchanging a word.

Suddenly, the train goes into a tunnel and everything is dark for several seconds... The sound of a kiss is heard in the darkness, followed by a loud slap. Then the train is out of the tunnel and they all look at each other. The Argentinian is blushing bright red, with a hand to his cheek. The Brazilian is smirking, barely controlling a laugh. Both women look indignant.

The elderly woman is thinking. "This is outrageous! While we were in that tunnel, this Argentinian fellow must have kissed the young lady and she slapped him on the face! Well done!"

The young lady is thinking: "Unbelievable! While we were in that tunnel, this Argentinian guy must have tried to kiss me, but in the dark he kissed this elderly woman by mistake and she smacked him on his face! Serves him right!"

The Argentinian is thinking: "This is crazy! In the dark, this Brazilian must have kissed the young lady; she swung at him but hit me instead! I got slapped for what the Brazilian did, and I didn't do anything!"

The smirking Brazilian is thinking: "This is hilarious! In the dark, I kissed my own hand loudly; then I smacked the Argentinian right in the face and everyone is trying to figure out what happened!"

A lot of assumptions are made, based on scarce information. These assumptions are usually wrong, especially in cross-culture situations.

In this case, an individual took advantage of this; in real life that kind of thing seldom happens.

40. The Survey in the Middle East

An American meat distribution company did a market survey to test the potential demand for pork meat, a product they intended to sell in the region. The survey was a disaster.

The researchers in Iraq asked: "Excuse me, what is your opinion about eating pork?"

The typical response they got was: "I'm sorry, I don't understand your question... what is "pork?"

The researchers in Ethiopia asked: "Excuse me, what is your opinion about eating pork?"

The typical response they got was: "I'm sorry, I don't understand your question... what is "eating?"

The researchers in Iran asked: "Excuse me, what is your opinion about eating pork?"

The typical response they got was: "I'm sorry, I don't understand your question... what is "opinion?"

The researchers in Israel asked: "Excuse me, what is your opinion about eating pork?"

The typical response they got was: "I'm sorry, I don't understand your question... what is "excuse me?"

When working across cultures, even questions can be misunderstood, not just statements. And if the question is misunderstood, the answer you get may lead you to the wrong conclusion: not because of the answer per se, but because the question was misinterpreted. Make sure that your question is free of culture bias before you go around asking it.

41. The Sheep in the Saloon

In a remote mining town deep in Peru, there were no women at all, just men. They were all there seeking fortune, looking for silver in the hills and panning for gold in the creeks. Mostly they spent their nights camping out wherever they were prospecting and eventually they would come into town for supplies, including booze.

One of these miners was a young Australian. He, too, had traveled a long way looking to become rich. It was his first endeavor in mining, so he was a bit inexperienced.

The first time he came into the town saloon after three weeks out on the hills, he was looking for a whore, but there weren't any. He questioned the bartender:

"No whores?! I can't believe it! How can you guys get along without any women at all?"

"Well, most of us end up doing it with an animal... You know, sheep, cows, pigs..."

"Yuk!" exclaimed the Aussie. "That's disgusting! I'll never do it with an animal!"

"Never say never, mate," pondered the bartender.

The Australian went back to the hills prospecting and returned to town again after another four weeks. This time he was so horny he was ready to do it with anything, animal, plant or mineral... He figured that all he had to do to overcome his disgust was to get really drunk, then he would be able to do it.

On his way to the saloon he saw a nice looking sheep grazing on an empty lot. He grabbed it under his arm and walked resolutely to the bar.

"Bar tender!" he yelled as he walked in. "Give me a bottle of whisky to go!"

There was a deep silence over the saloon. Everybody stopped what they were doing and stared at him.

"What are you staring at, you hypocrites? I know you all do it with animals, too!"

"Yes," said an old guy next to the door. "But what you got there is the Sheriff's mistress!"

When in a foreign land, make sure you understand the rules of the local culture and to what situations they apply. Avoid acting before checking with a local if you are really doing the right thing in the specific situation.

42. Dancing to the Music

This is a true story that happened to friends of mine.

There was this couple who loved to travel and loved to dance. Since they first met, many years before, they often went out dancing; and often they were the first couple on the floor, as soon as the band started to play.

One night they found themselves in Germany, having joined one of those "Berlin by Night" tours. As a part of a group of some twenty people, they were taken on a mini-bus to see some of the city's monuments lit by floodlights; then they were taken to dinner at a typical restaurant, and afterwards to a nightclub.

As they settled at their table in the nightclub, a live band started playing a jazzy tune. Loyal to their own tradition, the couple left the table and they were the first ones on the dance floor, dancing a fox-trot to the music.

As soon as they did that, however, the band stopped playing. The couple felt a little awkward... They noticed that they were the only ones on the dance floor, and that the band members were staring at them. They decided to go back to their table and have the drinks that had just been served to them as part of the tour.

No sooner had they sat down, the band started playing exactly the same tune, from the beginning. This time, the couple decided to wait and see if others would begin dancing.

Then a young woman emerged from backstage and started to dance sexily in front of the band, slowly removing her clothes as she did so... They had unwittingly spoiled the beginning of a strip-tease act!

When you are in a strange culture, you are often told to "dance according to the music." Just be sure that you understand the situation before you start dancing when you are not supposed to dance... Maybe the music is intended for something else!

43. Rabbi and Priest Intimate Talk

A Jewish rabbi and a Catholic priest preached in a village whose inhabitants were about evenly spread between the two religions. The community was peaceful and the people often collaborated with each other; the differences in their beliefs were not an obstacle to the villagers' co-existence. Over the years, the two men of God also developed a personal friendship, confiding in each other.

On one particular evening, after sharing a modest meal, they sat together talking in front of a small fireplace that mitigated the rigors of a harsh winter.

Rabbi – You know, my friend, after all these years, I've learned that there are more things in our religions that bring us together, rather than things that push us apart.

Priest – I agree, dear friend. God almighty is merciful, and He has shown us that His love can take different names and be expressed in different rituals, but above all His love shines equally for all of us.

Rabbi – You are right; the differences are more in the rituals we apply and less in the essence of worshipping the Lord above. For instance, I am forbidden to eat pork; yet I am allowed to take a wife. You, on the other hand, are forbidden to marry and to have sex; yet you are allowed to eat pork with no restrictions...

Both men sat in silence for a while, meditating and looking at the fire. Then the priest spoke, hesitantly.

Priest – Please forgive my curiosity, my friend. May I dare to ask you a very personal question?

Rabbi – Of course you may. What do you wish to know?

Priest – In all these years, have you ever disobeyed the rules of your religion and tried eating pork, just to experience what it was like?

Rabbi – (taking a deep breath) Well, to you I can say this my friend, because I know you will treat this with discretion. Yes, I did eat pork once in my life. I was young and I wanted to know what it tasted like, so I ate pork. And now I know.

They sat in silence for a while longer. Then the Rabbi spoke slowly.

Rabbi – And what about you, my friend? Have you ever broken your chastity vows and had sex?

Priest – (clasping his hands together and looking at the floor) Yes, I must confess that I did, once. I was young and I met this beautiful woman who I could not resist. We had sexual relations one night, and then we never saw each other again.

The men were quiet again for a long while, looking at the flames. Then the Rabbi broke the silence with a whisper to his colleague:

Rabbi – Sex is better than pork...

Religion is a delicate subject for humor, especially across cultures. Be very careful in assessing whether your audience (one person, ten people or one hundred) is likely to see the humor in what you are going to tell them. People need to be open to looking at their own religion and having a bit of fun with it.

Having said all this, the story above is one of those rare items that I've found to be appreciated by all who have heard it.

44. Argentinian Expat in Spain

An Argentinian had been living in political exile in Spain for over ten years. He started feeling a sort of cultural identity crisis, so he consulted a psychoanalyst.

Argentinian – Doctor, I think I am losing my mind... I am losing my national identity as an Argentinian! The other day, I felt like going out to dinner and having a juicy steak made on a "parrilla." But when I got to the restaurant, before I knew it, I ordered "paella" instead...

Doctor – OK, tell me more...

Argentinian – Last week, I invited my wife to go dancing, so we were looking for a nightclub where we could dance a tango. But we wound up in a different place, and before I knew it, I was dancing a flamenco!

Doctor – Don't worry, this is a condition we can take care of by using hypnosis. I will hypnotize you, and this will help you recover your sense of identity as an Argentinian. Look closely at this watch that I am swinging in front of you like a pendulum: you are getting sleepy, you will close your eyes and go into a deep, deep slumber... Now repeat after me: "I am Argentinian..."

Argentinian – I am Argentinian...

Doctor – I will count to three, and when I snap my fingers, you will wake up and you will feel that you are indeed an Argentinian... One, two, three! (Snaps his fingers). So, how do you feel?

Argentinian – It's none of your business, you shitty Spaniard!

Argentinians have a reputation for being arrogant and having big egos. As is usual with all stereotypes, the less you know the persons involved, the more you tend to rely on stereotypes to guide your own thinking. I have an Argentinian friend who actually enjoys collecting and spreading jokes about Argentinians... I suppose this is a way of downplaying the underlying resentment that some people feel against specific individuals who may have behaved badly in certain situations.

45. The Slobonians and the Matchboxes

This is another one of those ethnic stories in which "Slobonian" is a nationality that you may choose to replace with the nationality you are most fond of teasing and stereotyping as being stupid.

The Brazilian (also replaceable by a nationality of your preference) Foreign Affairs Minister was visited by the Slobonian Ambassador, who wished to express a complaint. The Ambassador said:

"Something needs to be done about these jokes that are circulating everywhere, always portraying the Slobonian people as stupid an incompetent. They are totally offensive and unjustified!"

The Brazilian Minister tried to handle this diplomatically:

"Look, there is no point in us arguing about this. Why don't we go out on the city and take a look at what is happening on the streets, in daily life, the two of us together?"

The Ambassador agreed and soon they were walking down the sidewalk on a busy avenue. They stopped in front of a bar called "Lisbon". The Minister said:

"Let's go in here. Let me do the talking, and just observe what happens."

They came to the counter and the Minister asked for a box of matches. The guy behind the counter handed him one, which the Minister examined, opened, and then remarked:

"These have all the matches organized pointing to the right side of the box... I'm looking for matches pointing to the left side."

The bartender apologized: "I'm sorry, sir, but all the matches we have are like this."

The men left and took to the streets again. They came upon another shop with a sign that read: "Coimbra Tobacco & Cigarettes". They went in and repeated the routine. The Minister asked for a box of matches, while the Ambassador observed.

"This box has all the matches pointing to the right side of the box... I'm looking for matches pointing to the left side," said the Minister.

"Sorry, sir, but all the matches we have are like this," responded the shopkeeper.

The men left, the Ambassador frowning and the Minister barely disguising a smile on his face. As they resumed their walk, they came to an establishment with a sign that read "Bar Rio de Janeiro".

Once again the Minister asked for a box of matches. The flamboyant bartender swiftly reached into a drawer and produced a matchbox, laying it on the counter with a perky "There you are!"

"This has all the matches organized pointing to the right side of the box... I'm looking for matches pointing to the left side."

The bartender responded: "No problem, sir, give me two seconds." He took the matchbox under the counter, away from his clients' view, and switched the box around, so that the matches were now pointing to the left side.

"This is what you want!" he asserted, putting the box on the counter. "All the matches pointing to the left side."

"Yes," agreed the Minister. "This is 50 cents, right?"

"Ah, no Sir," contested the bartender. "These matches are special, each box is 75 cents!"

They paid the bartender and left. Once outside, the Minister turned to the Ambassador:

"You see, my friend, the stories people tell are not an unfair prejudice, they are not fiction. You have just seen that they reflect reality..."

"I am forced to agree with you," said the Ambassador reluctantly. "None of the Slobonians was able to secure the new product!"

This story highlights the naiveté of the Slobonians and also the unethical smartness of that last bartender, who took advantage of that naiveté. These roles are often played out between different nationalities, especially involving certain cultures who like to think of themselves as "smarter" than the guys across the border, or sometimes involving colonized countries who enjoy making fun of the Northern cultures that dominated them in the past.

Humor can be used as a very damaging weapon and can be very hurtful; it always depends on which side of the joke you are on!

46. Three Kinds of Hell

An investment banker died and went straight to Hell, flying Business Class. When he got there, a demon receptionist explained that after some reorganization carried out by a consulting firm, Hell was divided into three sections, each of them outsourced to a different nationality. New arrivals were asked to choose among the three options.

"Behind the first door," explained the receptionist, "you have American Hell. Everyday you will get an hour of electric shocks on a chair, two hours burning in a cauldron over a stove and 10 lashes from a torturer. Behind the second door you will reach German Hell: there you will get two hours on the electric chair, three hours in the burning cauldron, and 20 lashes from the torturer."

The banker was not impressed. The receptionist continued:

"Behind the third door lies the Brazilian Hell: there you will stay for three hours on the electric chair, four hours in the burning cauldron, and you will receive 30 lashes from the torturer."

The investment banker moaned: "Each one is worst than the previous one…"

The receptionist whispered to him: "Take the Brazilian Hell: the electric chair is out of order and nobody knows how to fix it; there's a shortage of gas for the stove; and the torturer never shows up for work!"

This is a very popular joke in Brazil. It reflects criticism by many Brazilians who would like to see things working more efficiently and effectively. Like most ethnic jokes, people will appreciate it if it's being told by a fellow national to a national audience. "We can all laugh together about our culture!"

However, it will not be appreciated if the same story is told by a foreigner, or if there are foreigners in the audience. Many people will then perceive it as harsh criticism, rather than as light-hearted humor.

47. When Is It Corruption?

This is a real case and all names have been changed to protect the privacy of the real people involved.

A construction company was involved in a series of long-term projects for the Military. Over the years, many small, medium and large projects were bid for and awarded to this same company, and a personal, informal relationship developed between a local Military Commander and the company's local Relationship Manager. This eventually resulted in the Commander (Colonel Guilherme) trusting the construction company RM (Bob de Bilder) completely, to the point of circumventing protocol.

Every month, when payments from the Government were due to be made to the company, the funds were available to Colonel Guilherme on the first day of the month. Protocol mandated that the company should submit a report describing detailed progress on each project; this report would usually be ready by the 7th day of the subsequent month. Guilherme and his staff would then carefully review the report, verify if the progress described was indeed true to form, and then make the payments (usually around the 15th).

Bob eventually arranged with Guilherme that he would get an advancement of 80% on the first day of the month; once the progress report was submitted, checked and approved or amended, the resulting balance would be paid out on the 15th.

This cozy arrangement went on for months, until one day Guilherme was promoted to another rank in a different city. He was replaced by Colonel Gilberto.

On the first day of the month, Bob dropped by the new Colonel's office to introduce himself and tried to quickly take off from where he had left things with Guilherme.

"I'd like to confirm that we can expect to receive our advancement today, as usual, since it's the first day of the month..." he said tentatively.

"What advancement?" asked Gilberto, sounding surprised and annoyed.

Bob explained the arrangement he had with the previous incumbent, and Colonel Gilberto became increasingly annoyed and agitated. At one point he interrupted Bob:

"This is highly irregular! I would say that this is actually criminal!" He called out to his assistant: "Put this man under arrest immediately! I need to investigate this situation."

To make a long story short, Bob spent the night in jail at the barracks; he was released next morning and an official inquiry into the matter was started.

Humiliated, Bob called his company's CEO and reported what happened. The president summoned him to company HQ for a meeting on the following day.

Once there, Bob presented a detailed account of everything relating to the company's relationship with the military unit involved; he apologized for mismanaging the situation with the new Commander and offered his resignation.

The CEO listened patiently to his whole presentation and then said: "Bob, I won't accept your resignation, and I'll give you a challenge: you have to make friends with this new Commander guy, you have to become his 'compadre'"! (In Latin cultures a "compadre" is someone who is a godfather to a friend's child.)

Bob was glad to hear that he could keep his job, but he could not see it possible to become friends with a Commander who had just thrown him in jail two days ago...

He went to see the Commander and apologized profusely. However, Colonel Gilberto wouldn't even look him in the eye, and asked him to leave immediately after hearing his extensive apology.

Bob started researching the Commander's background, trying to find an angle that he could use to approach the Colonel with a different perspective. Eventually, he found out that Gilberto was a huge fan of football (soccer) and a big supporter of the local team "Sport Club Internacional".

Over the coming weeks, he started to play that angle.

Bob visited the Commander practically every week and often talked about football; he asked the Commander's opinion about the latest games, the prospects for the coming matches, how Internacional was doing in the national championship, etc.

In one of these visits, he asked the Commander: "Colonel, I hear that you're also quite a football player?"

"I sometimes play on week-ends with the officers, just to keep in shape..." he replied modestly.

"From what I've heard, you're being very modest! They tell me you're the best guy on the team!"

"No, that's an exaggeration... There are others who play just as well as I do."

"I know that you are a fan of Internacional: what would you say if you had the opportunity to join them in a training session, for an afternoon during the week?"

The Colonel could not hide a sparkle in his eyes, but said nothing. Bob continued: "I have a close friend who is part of their Management Team. I will see what is possible to arrange."

Bob was the quintessential relationship manager; he got along with everybody and had friends everywhere. He was often behind the scenes at the Internacional club, where he sat on the Advisory Board. He arranged for Colonel Gilberto to take part in an internal training match that happened every week at the Internacional training grounds, in which the main team played 45 minutes against the reserves. Just before the session, he assembled the players and gave them instructions: "Pass the ball to this guy at every opportunity! It's his birthday tomorrow and this will be a special treat!"

In summary: Colonel Gilberto had a great time, played alongside his sport idols and scored two goals in that training session. He was absolutely overjoyed! He talked about it for weeks and gradually developed a friendship with Bob.

A year later, he asked Bob to be the godfather to his newborn son at his baptism ceremony.

In this company, this story has been told many times as a model of how relationship managers should behave. In Latin, African and Asian cultures, similar behavior is often stimulated and praised. However, in Germanic and Anglo-Saxon cultures, this might be seen as outright corruption, even though there was no exchange of money, no monetary bribe involved.

This is often a major challenge for international companies: how far are you willing to go when trying to adapt your conduct to local patterns of behavior? What do you consider corruption and what do you consider "a normal exchange of pleasantries?" Where do you draw the dividing line?

This is a good topic for debate.

48. Bribing the Goalkeeper

In a small town deep in the interior of Brazil, the local football championship (soccer to American ears) was coming to its climax with the big final match between Flamengo and Fluminense, or rather, the local versions of these two famous Rio teams.

The town was small, but it also had its share of organized crime. Two days before the big game, the goalkeeper of Fluminense, a player nicknamed "Moreno", was approached by a shady guy with a briefcase.

"Listen, pal," whispered the guy. "There's some people betting big money on the Sunday game. They're willing to pay you ten grand if you just… well, play badly. Drop a ball in an opponent's foot, you know… fail to make a save… You know what I mean."

"What," said Moreno indignantly. "You're asking me to risk my career for a measly ten grand?"

"OK. Tell you what… I'll double the offer. It will be twenty grand."

"What? Are you asking me to risk my career for just twenty thousand dollars?"

This went on for a few times more, until eventually they settled for fifty thousand.

Then came the time for the big game; the small town's stadium was packed. The game was evenly balanced between the two teams: a lot of scrimmaging in the midfield, few attacks, very few chances to score. At half time, the score was still a goalless tie.

The second half wore on, and still no score. With 15 minutes to go before the final whistle, a high ball is crossed over the Fluminense goal. True to his agreement, Moreno goes for it, fumbles it miserably and drops it right in front of the Flamengo striker; but the striker shoots it over the goal.

Two minutes later, Moreno again fumbles a save and the ball spills in front of another Flamengo attacker; the guy shoots it wide. In the last ten minutes, Moreno fumbles every ball he gets to touch; but each time, the Flamengo attackers miss their shots.

Finally, with one minute to go, a Flamengo attacker races towards the goal and Moreno jumps at his legs instead of at the ball. The referee calls a penalty kick.

As the striker runs to shoot the penalty, Moreno slips and falls on his face between the goal posts; the striker shoots wide and misses the open goal.

The match is over, a scoreless tie. The result means that Fluminense is the town league champion.

Moreno gets his fifty grand payment that evening. After all, he fulfilled his side of the bargain, playing the worst match he possibly could. It's not his fault that Flamengo wasted all the chances he gave them.

On the next day, Moreno keeps ten grand to himself; and he pays out ten grand to each of the four Flamengo attackers, for missing every shot they made against the Fluminense goal, as they had previously agreed, on the eve before the match!

At the time this story was first published, as a joke on a Brazilian newspaper, the author provided the following moral: "either we all become ethical, or let's all steal as much as we can!"

The story and the moral reflect a typical mindset of Collectivist societies, in which group norms are more important than individual standards and individual responsibilities. Being with the group (whether behaving ethically or unethically) is more important than "doing what is right."

This can be a major obstacle to eradicating corruption. It is necessary to create a widespread group commitment towards behaving ethically; otherwise any exception will be used as an excuse to tolerate (or engage in) corruption, "because the others are doing it." This is perhaps true in any society, but it is more pronounced in collectivist societies in comparison to individualist ones.

49. Test Review at School

This is a true story that happened in my family many years ago in Brazil. It illustrates how disputes are handled in a Collectivist culture like Brazil, though the principles involved are applicable to all Collectivist cultures.

It was the end of the school year and the little girl, ten years old, needed to get a grade of 7.0 on a scale of 0 to 10, on the last monthly test for the subject "Portuguese Language", in order to be allowed to pass to the next grade without having to do a lengthy exam. In those days, the school system allowed students with an average grade of 7.0 or above, to forego the yearly exam.

When she got her test results, she was distraught. Her grade on the test was 6.75! Because of a 0.25 gap, she would have to continue with daily lessons for another month, and then do the lengthy exam. She would surely pass the exam (the required passing grade was 5.0) but it meant an extra four weeks at school, while most of her friends would already be enjoying their summer vacation.

She brought home the test with the annotated corrections her teacher had made in red ink, and showed it to her mother, almost in tears.

Her mother comforted her and, being a former primary teacher herself, decided to review the mistakes her daughter had made. One of them caught her attention: it was a spelling mistake in a writing assignment. There was a word circled in red, and two small red "x's" marked above it, meaning two mistakes, at 0.25 each, had been subtracted from the overall maximum grade possible. She asked her daughter:

"Darling, did the teacher say what this is about?"

"Yes, said the little girl. She said there are two spelling mistakes in this word." (For the English readers' benefit, I have used an English language word equivalent). The word is "correct" and I wrote it "conrect". The teacher said that, in the sentence I wrote, this could be "connect", but then the "r" is wrong; and it could also be "correct", but then the "n" is wrong. So she counted two mistakes and discounted 0.5 points.

The mother was upset: "But this is wrong... It has to be considered either one way, or the other, but it should not be considered as two mistakes! I'm going to have a word with her."

The next day, while her daughter attended classes in other subjects, the mother managed to get the teacher aside during a free period and brought the issue to her attention. She excused herself to the teacher, stating that she normally would not argue over 0.25 points on a monthly test that her daughter did, but in this case it was important, since it might mean the difference between having four more weeks of school, plus the exam, and enjoying summer vacation starting next week.

The teacher, however, refused to concede on the matter. She insisted that there were, indeed, two mistakes in that one word and she saw no reason to change the grade she had awarded the pupil.

The mother decided to escalate:

"I find this unacceptable. Let's take the matter to the School Principal!"

"If that's what you want," replied the teacher, "let's do that. I'm sure she will back my criteria on this issue!"

They marched together to the office of the Principal, who was available to see them immediately. As they entered the office, the Principal recognized the mother as a former teacher at the same school, and a dear friend that she had not seen in years.

"Mary!" she exclaimed. "Where have you been hiding all these years? You never came by again to visit us!" They embraced and kissed each other twice on the cheeks.

"I'm sorry to bother you, Esther," said the mother. "Something came up in my daughter's Portuguese Language test and we need you to settle a disagreement I'm having with her teacher. I hope you don't mind..."

As the mother turned to the teacher, she suddenly realized that the teacher was no longer there... She had left the room, the minute she realized that the mother and the Principal were close friends.

The point here is not the outcome of the story (the daughter received her report card two days later with a grade of 7.0 for Portuguese Language on that month, therefore passing to the next grade without needing to do the exam). The point is that, in a Collectivist society, relationships are so important that the teacher gave up the discussion without even presenting her arguments to the Principal.

In her Collectivist mindset, she probably went into the office thinking "I'm sure to win this argument, because the Principal will back me up against this pupil's mother; it's a matter of the school staff standing beside each other against 'an outsider', the child's mother."

When she saw that the Principal and the mother were old friends, the situation was flipped. In her Collectivist mind, she had now become the outsider, since she did not enjoy such a close friendship with the Principal. In order to save face, she chose to simply leave quietly, without even defending her case.

In Collectivist cultures, issues are often resolved in light of the relationships among the people involved. The actual content of the issue is secondary.

50. Malay, Chinese and Indian at the Gates of Heaven

In Malaysia there are three predominant ethnic groups: the Malaysians themselves, the Chinese and the Indians. One day a member of each community died and the three of them found themselves standing in front of the Gates of Heaven.

They heard a loud voice coming from above and suddenly Saint Peter descended upon them and said: "We are a discrimination-free organization, we have no prejudice against Christians, Muslims, Buddhists or any religion whatsoever. However, starting this week, everyone must pay $ 100 to enter. You should pay at the cash desk right next to the gate."

What happened to the three of them?

None of them managed to get in.

The Chinese tried to bribe Saint Peter by offering him $50 directly to get in through the staff entrance; the Indian was bargaining over the price, and the Malay was waiting for the government to pay for his entry!

This story illustrates the stereotypes that exist among these three ethnic groups in Malaysia. I've used it to introduce the topic of stereotyping in that country. Sometimes, by offending all groups involved, in an equal manner, you may shock them into feeling empathy towards the others. The idea is to allow people to feel offended, to see what it's like to be discriminated against. Humor can be a good tool to start a serious conversation going, about mutual respect and about the underlying values in culture that trigger stereotyping and discrimination.

51. Englishman Drinking Water in India

Whenever the situation calls for a comment on stringent security measures, or some way of mitigating risk, I refer to this short story. Just something to lighten the mood and allow people to look at things in perspective

You should do as the English Colonel did when he was stationed in India: in order to avoid getting any kind of illness from the local water, he first put the water through a filter; then he boiled it for 10 minutes; then he filtered it again. Finally, he drank beer instead!

52. Education in a Hierarchical Culture

This was once told to me by a great friend from Portugal, but it applies equally to illustrate how education is perceived in any hierarchical, high Power Distance culture.

A little boy went to school for his very first day. When he came back, his father asked him:
"So, how was your first day at school?"
"So, so..." said the little boy sadly.
"Well, what happened?" asked the father.
"The teacher asked me how much was two and two..."
"And what did you say, my son?"
"I didn't say anything... I didn't know the answer!"
"You did well, my son. You are going there to learn, and not to teach!"

In high Power Distance cultures, the teacher takes the initiative and drives the learning process by lecturing to the pupils; these, in turn, are expected to adopt a rather passive attitude and try to absorb as much as possible the wisdom and knowledge that the teacher is giving to them as a gift, that they should accept and enjoy.

In low Power Distance cultures the teacher adopts a different role, as a facilitator, stimulating the students to take initiative, carry out research about certain subjects, and debate them in class.

53. Dinner Without Speaking the Language

The explosive growth in the Chinese economy brought with it a significant increase in international tourism for the Chinese people. Suddenly, people who had never been abroad could now afford to visit faraway places and very different cultures.

Our short story is about an elderly Chinese gentleman, a humble shopkeeper whose son made a fortune overnight designing apps for mobile phones. This prodigal son wanted his father to see the world, so he bought him a plane ticket to go to the US as a Birthday gift.

As our story begins, we find this elderly Chinese gentleman smack in the middle of New York. He is staying at the cheapest hotel he could find on the West side of Manhattan, does not speak a word of English, but he is eager to see the sights and learn about America.

When dinnertime comes, he finds a simple restaurant across the street from his hotel and goes there. The waiter shows him the menu, but he cannot understand a word of what is written there.

He sees that a couple on the next table order "spare ribs" and he decides to give it a go. He orders something that sounds like "spaaaruh reebuhs" and the waiter, miraculously, understands him and brings him a huge plate of pork ribs slathered in barbecue sauce. He enjoys his meal and eats far more than he is used to doing.

The next day we find him once more at the same place. He enjoyed the ribs, so he orders again: "spaaaruh reebuhs," and is pleased one more time.

On the third evening, however, he feels that he has had enough spare ribs to last him a lifetime; he decides to try something different, for a change. He sees someone at the next table ordering "a ham sandwich" and he likes the sound of it.

He motions to the waiter and asks for "a hamma sendweesh."

"Sure," says the miraculous waiter. "Would you like that on brown or white bread?"

The Chinese gentleman does not understand what in the world the waiter is saying, so he repeats his order, louder: "a hamma sendweesh!"

"Yes, but would you like that in brown or white bread?" asks the waiter, irritated.

The Chinese tries a different pronunciation: *"uh... hemma senduwitchuh?"*

"Yes!" shouts the waiter, losing his patience. *"But DO YOU WANT IT ON BROWN OR WHITE BREAD?" Everyone in the restaurant is looking at them and the Chinese gentleman feels like hiding under the table in shame.*

He moans: *"spaaaruh reebuhs..."*

When traveling abroad and not knowing the language, it is not enough to learn how to ask something; you also need to learn a little bit more so that you can understand the other person's reply! Or else you might get into more trouble than if you had not asked (or ordered) anything...

54. Two Nationalities in a Cruise Ship

Joaquim Oliveira is a middle-aged bachelor who goes on a week-long Mediterranean cruise. He is assigned to have his meals sharing a table with another bachelor of similar age, a gentleman from Germany. Both of them speak only their respective native languages: Portuguese and German.

When the time comes for them to have their first meal, the German is punctual, while the Portuguese arrives a few minutes later. When he comes to the table, the German is already there and the first course is already on their plates. The German is about to start eating, but when he sees the Portuguese gentleman arriving at the table, he politely stands up and greets him with a nod, saying "Guter Appetit!"

The Portuguese responds with a quick handshake and says "Joaquim Oliveira", introducing himself. They eat in polite silence, since their lack of a common language forbids them to have a dialogue.

At dinnertime, the same situation is repeated. When the Portuguese arrives, the German is already there. The latter once again stands up, clicks his heels and says politely "Guter Appetit!", to which the Portuguese once more replies with a curt handshake saying "Joaquim Oliveira".

Later in the evening, the Portuguese gentleman asks a crewmember: "That German gentleman who shares the table with me, can you tell me his name?"

"Certainly, that is Mr. Hans Waltmann, from Frankfurt"

"But he said something like 'Guter Appetit' before we sat down to eat..."

"He was using the German expression for 'have a nice meal'," responds the crewmember. "You know: like saying 'bon appétit' in French, or "bom apetite" in Portuguese."

The Portuguese gentleman realizes that he misunderstood his German fellow passenger and mistakenly introduced himself twice...

The next morning, for breakfast, he decides to make it up. He manages to arrive early at their table. When the German arrives, as usual, on time, the Portuguese is already there to greet him. He stands up politely, clicks his heels and says cheerfully: "Guter Appetit!"

To which the German replies, equally cheerful: "Joaquim Oliveira!"

When interpreting a situation involving different cultures, the best of intentions are often mistaken... And the misinterpretation works both ways: you misinterpret the other, they misinterpret you, and so on, endlessly, unless someone is able to break the cycle by stopping and asking short, open questions, really trying to understand the other before acting or saying anything else.

55. Know-how and Savoir-faire

Do you know the difference between "know-how" and "savoir-faire"? Curiously, both expressions have exactly the same meaning, when you look at the actual words. However, they mean very different things when taken as idiomatic expressions, as this story illustrates.

An American and a Frenchman died on the same day and reached the Pearly Gates of Heaven at the same time. Saint Peter was expecting them, in front of the gates, with some sad news.

"We've recently hired McKinsey consultants to restructure our organization, and this has resulted in a downsizing program. The bottom line is that we have just one opening available, while there are two of you aspiring to come in..." He paused for effect and then continued: "We've also been told by the consultants that we need to implement a meritocracy, to boost participation and to better empower people; therefore, I'll leave it up to you two, to sort it out for yourselves and decide who is more deserving of coming into Heaven. While you resolve this, I will wait inside; after 15 minutes I will come out again to see what you've decided."

The two men looked at each other rather puzzled. They were quickly distracted as they saw that Saint Peter was struggling to open the gates and get back inside Heaven.

"What's happening?" asked the Frenchman.

"I don't know what's wrong with this door," responded Saint Peter slightly annoyed. "I can't get it to open!"

The American went quickly into action: he reached into his shirt pocket and took out a handy pen, that was also convertible into a screwdriver and into a LED flashlight; he started working on the lock, trying to get the gate open. After a minute or two of fumbling, the lock clicked and the door swung open.

"Yess! I did it!" celebrated the American, clenching his fist in a pumping motion.

"Thank you," said Saint Peter. "I guess you deserve to go into heaven, for what you've just done."

"Wait," interrupted the Frenchman. "Are you going to allow a lock-picker to go into heaven?..."

The American had know-how; but the Frenchman had "savoir-faire"!

In a humorous manner, this story illustrates the stereotypes of the American and the French cultures. Beyond the stereotypes, it also illustrates some underlying values of those cultures, reflected in the respective languages through these two idiomatic expressions.

"Know-how" is about technical expertise, performance, knowing how to do things, having a bias for decisive action, deliberate behavior towards a clear short-term goal. These are underlying values of the American culture.

"Savoir-faire" is about diplomacy, etiquette, knowing what is the most elegant thing to do in order to achieve an ultimate objective, through indirect communication, by suggesting, implying, or asking polite questions that will, by indirect means, allow you to reach your objective. These are underlying values of the French culture.

PART VI – LEARNING

56. The Speed of Light

Learning is something that comes from experience, and as such, can happen in different ways to different people, depending on the different experiences that they have accumulated in their lives, as this story illustrates.

In a television quiz show on cable TV, three contestants were competing: a Russian, an American, and a Slobonian (these Slobonians are everywhere...)

The show host asked them this question: "What is the fastest thing in the world?"

As the clock ticked, the Russian gave his response: "It's 'thought'! Nothing beats the speed of just thinking a thought!"

The American exclaimed: "It's the speed of light! Nothing is faster than the speed of light!"

Then it was the Slobonian's turn. He frowned and scratched his head, looking for an answer. Then his eyes lit up and he hit the palm of his hand on the pulpit in front of him. "There is something that is faster than thought, and faster than light... It's diarrhea!" He exclaimed joyfully.

"Diarrhea?" asked the astonished TV host.

"Yes," explained the Slobonian. "When you've got diarrhea, you just have to go to the toilet so fast, there is no time to think, no time to even turn on the light!"

57. Cavalry Recruits

Learning can be very challenging, as demonstrated by a military cavalry instructor I once met. In Brazil, young men who turn 18 are obliged to enlist for military service lasting one year. In the 60's (I'm not sure how it works today), if they were already in college, they could opt for a few months of cavalry training on weekends and half-day week-days, in order to continue their studies at the same time.

At the first training session with a group of new recruits, the instructor called out: "Whoever has never mounted a horse before, take a step forward!" Half the group of shy young men took a step forward. The instructor continued: "Very well. Now over here to the left we have a group of horses who have never been mounted before. You will all learn together!"

In different cultures there are different approaches to learning. Depending on the circumstances, "learning with each other" may not be the best approach... This works well in North America and Northern Europe (mostly egalitarian cultures), but will not work well in hierarchical cultures, which predominate in Southern Europe and in most other countries.

Also, the approach to learning in Anglo-Saxon and North European cultures tends to be more pragmatic, emphasizing opportunities for pupils to "learn by themselves" and learn through "experiential learning". This means first experiencing a situation, or discussing a case, and only after this practical experiencing receive explanations from the professor/teacher about the underlying theoretical concepts involved.

In hierarchical cultures, by contrast, learning is centered on the teacher, rather than on the pupils. The teacher/professor starts with a lecture, or with a conceptual explanation, and only after that, invites his students to engage in discussions or participate in an exercise applying the concepts presented by the professor.

58. Three Nuns at the Pearly Gates

Sometimes you may know the answer to a question without even realizing that you do, as illustrated by this story.

Three nuns died and came to the Pearly Gates of Heaven at the same time. As they were about to cross the gates, Saint Peter appeared and stopped them.

"Not so fast, my dear sisters. We've been getting a lot of criticism towards the Catholic Church, lately; so we'll need to make you go through a small test, to verify if you are indeed devout Catholics and you know your scriptures."

The three sisters chattered nervously, and one of them, who was the most talkative of the three, turned to Saint Peter and asked:

"What happens if we don't know the answer to your questions?"

"I will ask you each a different question, one at a time," he explained. "If your response is correct, the gates of Heaven will open automatically for the respondent. If you get the wrong answer, a chute will open beneath your feet and you will go straight to Hell!"

"Oh my!" exclaimed the talkative nun, increasingly nervous.

"Who will go first?" asked Saint Peter.

"I want to go last," said the talkative nun. One of the other two stepped forward.

Saint Peter said: "Here is your question: who was the first man created by God?"

"Oh, that's an easy one!" exclaimed the nervous nun.

"Adam," said the first nun. Trumpets were heard: "tadaa!" and the gates swung open, closing after the first nun went through.

The second nun stepped forward. Saint Peter asked:

"What was the name of the first woman created by God?"

"Oh, that's an easy one!" exclaimed the nervous nun.

"Eve," said the second nun. Trumpets blared "tadaa!" and the gates swung open, closing after she had gone inside.

"Now it's your turn," said Saint Peter to the third nun. *"What was the first thing that Eve said to Adam when she saw him for the first time?"*

"Oh, that's a hard one!" exclaimed the nervous nun. *"Tadaa!"* Blared the trumpets and the gates swung open for her.

59. Englishman Training a Camel

When training people it is important not to put them under too much pressure. Putting some pressure on your pupils is OK, it may even be motivating, sometimes, but you need to avoid overdoing it, as this short tale illustrates.

An Englishman was stationed in North Africa during World War II and decided to use a camel for reconnaissance work in the desert. He had read in London that camels could go without water in the desert for as much as 40 days.

However, he observed that his particular camel would drink water on a daily basis. He decided that he needed to train the camel to extend the amount of days it could go without water. So he started stopping the camel from drinking, so that it would get used to a longer period without water.

First he left the camel without water for a week, and then allowed it to drink. Next he kept the camel without water for two weeks. He gradually increased the period without water for the camel, and as it was almost reaching 40 days without water, the camel died of thirst...

Some trainers put such a strong emphasis on challenging their students, that they overdo it to the point of demotivating and frustrating them. Challenge works better as a motivating factor in performance-oriented cultures such as the Anglo-Saxons, Germanic, Japanese and Chinese. In caring cultures such as the Scandinavians, or in many Latin cultures, challenge needs to be fine-tuned very carefully so as not to exceed a threshold, beyond which it has the opposite effect.

60. Teaching a Dog to Pee Outside

A man was reading his newspaper, sitting on his favorite chair in his living room, when the dog his wife had recently bought came beside him, raised its hind leg and peed on the side of the chair.

The man's immediate impulse was to strike the dog with his newspaper; but this man was a teacher, so he resisted the impulse and decided to teach the dog the right behavior.

He went outside to his back yard and took the dog with him to a tree that they had there. Making sure that the dog was still looking at him intently, the man opened his trousers and peed on the tree, saying: "See? This is what you should do!"

He went back to his favorite chair and resumed reading his paper. With one corner of his eye he observed the dog, curious to see what it would do.

After a while the dog came into the living room, walked to where the man was sitting, stood on his hind legs and peed again on the chair! But this time, he used the same position that the man had demonstrated when peeing on the tree!

The moral of this story is that people (and dogs) learn what they want to learn, and not necessarily what someone else is trying to teach them. Learning is always selective, and it depends on what the learner chooses to learn.

This story is best told with exuberant body language, adopting the dog's posture in each situation. Actual peeing in front of your audience is not recommended.

61. Detailed Instructions

Giving detailed instructions are not a guarantee that people will do what is necessary, especially when it involves the elderly.

An old lady had invited her friends to tea. However, since she was becoming quite forgetful, she asked her daughter to help her out.

The daughter was a busy executive of a major investment bank, so she couldn't just skip work for an afternoon to have tea with her mother and friends, but she tried to help as best as she could.

She came by her mother's during her lunch break and prepared everything, then called the old lady into the kitchen:

"Look mum, I've left everything ready, right here on the kitchen counter: a tray with the tea cups; a second tray with biscuits; and a third tray with chocolate truffles. And I've written what you need to do on this post-it, stuck on the refrigerator door: 1) serve tea; 2) serve biscuits; 3) serve chocolate truffles."

"Thank you so much dear," said the old mother. "Don't worry, everything will be fine!"

The busy executive went off to ripping off her clients, and the mother sat down and waited for her guests to arrive. When they did, she invited them to sit around the dining room table and went to the kitchen to fetch the tea.

They sat and had tea, chatting happily about their families and the latest happenings on the local TV soap opera. After a while, the old lady remembered that there was something more that she was supposed to do... what was it?

She went into the kitchen and saw the post-it note on the fridge. "Ah!" she said to herself. "Serve tea!" So she got more tea bags and served more tea to her guests. After another half-hour, she got that feeling again that she was forgetting something...

She went into the kitchen again and saw the post-it note on the fridge door. "Ah!" she said to herself. "Serve tea!" So she once again got more tea bags and served more tea to her guests.

After a couple of hours of this, the guests gently excused themselves and left. They had had too much tea and nothing to eat...

When evening came, the busy daughter dropped by to check if everything had gone all right. She walked into the kitchen and saw the trays with biscuits and chocolates on the kitchen counter, untouched, just as she had left them.

"Mother, what happened? You didn't serve the biscuits nor the chocolates to your friends?"

"My dear, you know what? They didn't come..."

62. Chinese Speaking Yiddish

Learning has everything to do with the environment, as this tale illustrates, having been told to me by a Jewish friend.

An Orthodox Jew visiting New York for the first time goes to a small Jewish restaurant in the heart of the Jewish district that had been recommended by a friend. As he sits at a table, he is surprised to see that the waiter looks like a young Chinese boy. His surprise is even greater when the boy addresses him in perfect Yiddish!

He orders, finishes his meal, and then sees that the owner of the place is coming to see him and ask if everything was to his liking.

"Yes, everything was perfect, thank you. But, tell me, how did you come across that nice Chinese boy as a waiter?"

"Well," says the owner, "actually he was abandoned at our doorstep as a baby. We raised him ever since and taught him everything he knows."

"That's wonderful! And he can speak perfect Yiddish!"

"Not so loud, please... He thinks it's English!"

This story pokes fun at how closed a Jewish community can be, even in the middle of Manhattan! And it also points to the fact that learning can be directed towards questionable goals... It's important to look at the context and the purpose of learning, not just at the content and at the teacher-learner relationship.

63. The Difference Between Psychologists and Psychiatrists

The difference between the attitudes of Psychologists and Psychiatrists is illustrated by this brief story:

At a national convention on the psychopathology of interpersonal relations, a Psychologist and a Psychiatrist cross each other in a corridor.
The Psychologist says "Hi!" and hurries along to the next lecture.
The Psychiatrist nods in return and continues on his path towards a different conference room.
The Psychiatrist thinks: "Hmm... I wonder what he meant by that?..."
The Psychologist thinks: "Hmm... I wonder what I meant by that?..."

The stereotype is that Psychologists are typically questioning themselves a lot, they are full of self-doubt and tend towards introspection. They are the personification of the famous philosopher's phrase: "All I know is that I know nothing!."

By contrast, Psychiatrists (according to the stereotype) are typically more self-confident, perhaps even to a fault. They tend to be analytical and critical of others, but not of themselves.

64. Missing the Flight

This story actually happened, involving members of my family, and it illustrates the opportunities for learning through coaching.

A few years ago one of my daughters, then 18 years old, went to Spain on a holiday for a week with her boyfriend. On the day they were due to fly back to our home in Amsterdam, we received an unexpected phone call, which my wife picked up. It was our daughter calling from a Spanish airport.

"Mom, we lost our flight! What can I do?"

"Calm down, dear; we'll sort it out. What happened?"

"Well, we arrived at the airport kind of early for our 1 pm flight, about an hour and a half in advance. So, we decided to have lunch before we checked in. We had lunch at this sandwich place at the airport, and then we went to look for the counter to check in. That's when we found out that we were at the wrong terminal! By then it was already after twelve and we had less than an hour... So we had to get a shuttle bus to get to the other terminal, but we waited for, like, 15 minutes before the bus showed up; then it took us another fifteen minutes for the bus to get to the other terminal, and then by the time we got to the right check-in counter the flight was closed! We were just a couple of minutes late, they had just closed it! We pleaded and pleaded, but they wouldn't let us board! And we had one of those saver tickets that won't allow us to get another flight! What can I do?"

And my wife, who is also a consultant and a certified coach, calmly asked: "OK dear, so what did you learn from this?"

With an irritated sigh, my daughter replied: "Next time, we should check in first, and then have lunch."

"Very good. Now what are your options? What could you do?"

"We tried to use our ticket to take another flight; however, they said that we need to pay a penalty for making such a change, and the penalty is practically the price of a new ticket..."

"So?..."

"Well, we don't have the money to pay for it... Can you help us with that?"

"OK, just go to the ticket counter and buy another ticket, using our credit card. We'll pay for it, don't worry. Call me when you have your new arrival time, we'll pick you up at the airport."

Managers are often confronted with problems brought to their attention by a staff member. What is usually expected is that the manager will provide a quick solution, directing the employee to solve the issue. However, these situations typically offer an opportunity to help the staff member to learn how to solve the problem, so that the next time something similar happens, he or she can resolve the issue without depending on the manager. Essentially, this is what coaching is: helping a person to use her/his own resources to solve a problem and learning in the process.

Managers should resist the impulse to provide a quick solution (if the situation is of a type that allows you to spend a few minutes in coaching). When your priority, as a manager, is to develop the staff member, opt for coaching rather than "putting out the fire."

As a manager, it is always up to you to assess the situation in an instant and decide: "should I coach or should I solve this? Should I give this guy a fish or should I take the opportunity and teach him how to fish?" If the situation allows it, go for coaching; this will develop the staff member's skills, allow him to grow, and he will not need to bother you next time a similar situation arises.

PART VII – CAREER DEVELOPMENT

65. At the Zoo

A new young lion arrives at the zoo. He sees that he has been put in a large cage next to another cage with another lion, much older than he is.

When the zoo opens for the public, a crowd gathers to see the new lion that has been advertised in the media. The young lion gives them a good show: he roars loudly, jumps around in his compound, walks about looking proud and kingly. The crowd cheers when he roars, more and more people come to see him.

Next door, the old lion spends the whole day lying lazily on a rock; he doesn't roar at all, doesn't jump, he just lies down and does nothing at all.

When feeding time comes, the zookeepers throw the old lion a couple of huge, juicy steaks. When they get to the young lion's cage, they leave him a bunch of bananas.

Bananas? The young lion is first confused, then outraged. He figures this must be a trick that they play on newcomers, some kind of initiation rite.

The next day, the young lion is even springier than the day before: he struts around briskly, he jumps on a pile of rocks, then down again; he roars so loudly that he can be heard a mile away and scares other animals in the zoo. The crowd going to see him gets even bigger: everybody wants to see this amazing feline who is so active and vigorous.

Next door, the old lion seems unfazed: he just yawns once in a while and goes back to sleep.

At the end of the day, at feeding time, the zookeepers give the old lion a couple of enormous steaks and throw a bunch of bananas to the young lion.

Bananas again? He doesn't understand what's going on and decides to swallow his pride and seek advice from the old timer next door:

"Hey, old man, you gotta help me out here… what's going on? I'm putting on the best show this zoo has ever seen, and all I get is a bunch of bananas? That does not make any sense! And all the while you're just sitting around doing nothing, but you get juicy steaks? Tell me, what do I need to do to get proper food?"

"You've got it all wrong, kid," says the old lion calmly. "This has nothing to do with performance, or merit. This is a public zoo; it's managed by the state government, by civil servants. No meritocracy whatsoever."

"So, how come I get bananas and you get steaks?" asks the young lion.

"It's simple," replies the old timer. "The zoo management wanted to get a new lion, but they didn't have the budget for a second lion. They did have the budget for another monkey. So you are actually a lion in a monkey budget!"

This is actually a rather common situation in the civil service... You can spot many "lions in monkey budgets", trying to do what they think is the best, but being discouraged by budget restrictions that will not support what they are trying to do. Day-to-day reality often does not fit with what you can read in the formal budget documentation!

66. Engineer In a Monkey Costume

This story refers to unemployment and how sometimes people with good qualifications are forced to take on less demanding jobs simply because those are the only jobs available.

An engineer found himself the victim of a downsizing program in a recessive economy. Unemployed, he sought another job as an engineer for several weeks, to no avail. Running out of money, he started to look for any kind of job, anything that would allow him to avoid going hungry.

Walking around town, he came across a circus that had recently arrived. He decided to ask if there were any odd jobs available; circuses often employ locals as temporary workers, doing all kinds of simple tasks like cleaning up, feeding the animals... They were bound to have something that he could do.

The circus manager received him in his office, in a trailer. He said:

"Yes, I do have something for you. The guy who did this had a... hmm... an accident, and we need a replacement for tonight, the show is about to start. Follow me!"

They went into the big tent where a crowd was already sitting impatiently, waiting for the evening performance to begin. Behind the curtains, the manager handed the engineer a monkey costume.

"Get into this, go out on the ring and pretend you're a monkey. Climb that ladder on the right, all the way to the top of that pole, and walk on that tight rope that stretches to the opposite side of the ring to another pole. That's your show!"

The engineer was dumfounded... "Shit," he thought. "I was prepared to do anything, but wearing a monkey suit is humiliating! And I've never been on a tightrope before, what if I fall?"

"Hurry up! The music is starting, it's your cue to get out on the ring!" prodded the manager.

The guy put on the costume and went into the ring. The crowd cheered wildly.

"Ladies and Gentlemen," announced the circus manager. "Welcome to Zimbo Circus! Our first act is the amazing Kungo in a feat of skill and bravery!"

He picked up a whip and cracked it towards the engineer in a monkey suit.

"Get up on that pole!" he commanded, cracking the whip closer to the engineer's ass.

The guy climbed on the pole and looked down. He was at a height of 10 meters or so. If he fell, it probably wouldn't kill him, but he might break a few bones...

"Behold!" announced the manager. "Kungo will attempt to cross the ring on a tight wire, with no safety net! Instead of a net, below him he will have this!" He uncovered a large cage and opened it. Out came three lions, growling and staring hungrily at the monkey on the pole.

"Oh my God!" said the engineer to himself. "That crook didn't mention anything about lions!"

The circus manager took the whip and cracked it again, an inch away from the monkey's ass. He shouted:

"Go, Kungo! Go to the other side!"

The crowd cheered wildly.

The engineer started walking slowly, balancing himself on the rope. He slipped and fell, but managed to grab the rope with his hands. The crowd went wild. So did the lions, roaring and jumping at the hanging monkey, and missing him by just a few inches.

He started praying: "Oh Lord, please, please save me from this! If I survive I promise I will go to church every day for the rest of my life!"

Then one of the lions whispered to him: "Hey! It's all right! Just keep up the act! We're three lawyers in lion costumes!"

67. Killing a Lion Each Day

In many cultures people refer to a demanding job as being one in which you have to "kill a lion every day", symbolizing the fact that each and every day you have to do something extraordinary and difficult, and yet you need to keep doing that kind of thing continuously.

Gauchos, the South American cowboys of Argentina, Uruguay and Southern Brazil, are known for being bragging macho types, often exaggerating their own accomplishments... They talk of "killing lions every day" at work, but most of the time they are spending their days bragging about things they have never actually done. They spend a lot of time bragging and actually do much less than what they brag about.

This is the story of one such gaucho who was called on his bluff, one day.

The gaucho was out on a Safari with people coming from other parts of the world. They were all inexperienced, but the gaucho was the only one who did not admit it. When the guide asked who had any previous experience hunting lions, everyone confessed that this was their first time; except for the gaucho, who lied that he had done this several times before and proceeded to tell a tall story about the time when he killed a jaguar with his bare hands on a tree top.

During the first few days of the Safari, his companions were impressed and assumed that the frequent stories he told were true. Soon, however, they spotted some inconsistencies in the stories and realized that the guy was just bragging and lying through his teeth.

One day they stopped and set up camp around a hunting cabin sitting at the edge of a clearing in the jungle. The guide said that they would stay there for a few days, going out each day to hunt and returning to spend the night at the cabin.

On the first day out, they soon encountered a hungry lion, who surprised them jumping out of the bush. The guide had gone on a bit ahead of them, and the group panicked. They all ran back to the cabin, as fast as they could.

The gaucho climbed a tree like a rocket and the lion tried to reach him from below. It turns out that lions are not that good as tree climbers, so the gaucho appeared to be safe for the moment. However, the lion was circling the tree impatiently, trying to find a way up, as the gaucho clung to one of the branches and yelled for help.

The rest of the group were all inside the cabin, watching from a window.

Suddenly, the tree branch broke and the gaucho came down still clutching it, falling right on top of the lion! The animal was stunned, and the gaucho stood up and ran like crazy for the cabin.

The lion quickly recovered and was immediately behind the gaucho, right on his heels.

"Open up! Open the door and let me in!" shouted the gaucho as he ran towards the cabin in desperation.

Inside, the others debated what to do: "We have to open the door!" said one guy. "No! We can't!" said another. "The lion is so close to him they will both come inside and then we all die!"

"Open up, for God's sake!" yelled the gaucho out of breath, almost at the cabin. Then he tripped and fell flat on his face, just before the door. The 400-pound lion, running inches behind him, was not able to stop and hit the door at full force, knocking it down and landing right in the middle of the cabin among the other hunters.

The gaucho quickly stood up and shouted to the guys inside the cabin: "OK, cut this one up in steaks for supper, while I go and fetch another one!"

The moral of this tale is that sometimes to have success in your career you may need to act a bit like the gaucho, amplifying your achievements and not admitting your inexperience... Just be careful that you do not overdo it!

68. A Story with Three Morals

Once upon a time there was a field mouse that became friends with a cow. On the same farm there was also a cat, which the owner kept with the precise purpose of getting rid of the mice.

As could be expected, one day the cat was chasing the mouse all over the field. The mouse came to the cow and asked for help.

"Don't worry," she said. "I'll hide you in here." And she promptly dumped a huge pile of shit on top of him, covering him completely.

The cat had seen the mouse running towards the cow and was right beside her immediately.

"Where's that mouse?" inquired the cat impatiently.

"Mouse? I didn't see no mouse around here..." responded the cow.

The cat was suspicious; he started sniffing around the cow for clues. He got to the pile of fresh shit right behind the cow.

Meanwhile, the mouse had been holding his breath deep in the cow's shit pile. He figured that the cat must be gone by now, so he stuck his head out to see if the coast was clear. Just as he did that, the cat noticed something moving in the pile of shit and, with a swift feline movement, swept the mouse out in his claws. He cleaned the mouse in a bucket of water and ate him.

This story has three morals:
1) Not everybody who gets you into shit is your enemy;
2) Not everybody who gets you out of shit is your friend;
3) If you're in deep shit, just keep quiet and never stick your head out!

This story may be used to illustrate the three morals presented at the end. It serves to develop critical thinking and a more nuanced view of the world around us. Some constructive debate can be had around the third statement (*If you're in deep shit, just keep quiet and never stick your head out!*). Indeed, this is a social norm in many cultures. However, some points might be made against them: for instance, if you don't talk to anyone when you're feeling down, this may lead to severe depression. In caring cultures like The Netherlands and Scandinavia, talking about your problems is more generally accepted rather than, by comparison, in performance-oriented cultures like the Anglo-Saxons and Germanics.

69. Rabbit Succession

The patriarch of Rabbit Inc., a family business, concluded that his son had reached puberty and needed some coaching to follow in the footsteps of his father. He called him over for a meeting and showed him a string of female bunnies, sitting side by side in a row.

"Son, what we do here most of the time is… we make more bunnies! I'm going to show you how it's done."

He got behind a bunny and had sex with it as rabbits do; this means that in two seconds it was over.

"Did you see how it's done?"

The young rabbit nodded earnestly.

"OK, this is what we're going to do now: I'm going to start on the right side of this row and cover each of these bunnies moving to the left; you start on the left end of the row and cover them moving to the right; and we'll see which one of us can get to the opposite end first! Got it?"

"Yes sir!" said the young rabbit.

"Ready, set, go!" And they were off.

The young rabbit was going fast: "Excuse me; thank you. Excuse me, thank you. Excuse me, thank you. Sorry, dad! Excuse me, thank you…"

If you are planning your succession, it's great to prepare a younger professional to take over from you; just make sure he doesn't end up screwing you in the process!

PART VIII – CHANGE MANAGEMENT

70. Psychology and Change

How many psychologists do you need in order to change a lamp?

*Just one… But the lamp needs to really **want** to change!*

The point here is that real change needs to come from within… or so say most psychologists. "The door to change only opens from the inside, you cannot force it from the outside," goes another popular psychology saying.

The issue is: how can you get people to want to change, rather than forcing them to change out of fear, threats, or brute force.

Engagement and discretionary effort come from people who make free choices out of their own volition; and free choices can only be deemed truly "free" if they are informed choices, if people have access to all the pertinent information about the different available options and their consequences.

71. The Man In The Coat

This is an old fable by Aesop, the Greek storyteller and famous talk show host. It illustrates the greater power of warmth, affection and persuasion, over attempting to make changes using force and fear as motivation.

The North Wind and the bright Sun were having an argument about who was the most powerful. Each had their own strong arguments and none was able to convince the other. Then the North Wind saw a man walking down the road and he proposed a way to settle the argument once and for all.

"Do you see that man walking down the road? Let's use him to settle this. Whoever is able to remove his cloak will be recognized by the other as being the most powerful!"

And he proceeded to blow as hard as he could, almost knocking the man of his feet and almost succeeding in blowing the man's cloak of his back. However, the man managed to hang on to his cloak and wrap it around his body to protect himself from the strong wind.

The North Wind blew even harder, and even colder. Yet, the stronger he blew, the more the man cringed and held on to his cloak, leaning against the wind.

Finally, the North Wind grew tired and stopped blowing.

"OK, let's see you try it... Hah! If I could not do it, you will never be able to do it!"

The sun came out in full force and shone with all his warmth. Soon it was so warm that the man felt too hot and removed his cloak, sitting down under the shade of a tree to cool down.

The North Wind had to concede defeat and recognize that warmth can be more powerful than blowing strong.

This story also relates to the previous one about provoking change to happen from within. If we accept the notion that people will change only if they **want** to change, then the issue is "how do we get them to want to change?"

A different series of dilemmas may crop up, regarding whether engagement strategies to provoke change are tantamount to manipulation, or not. There is no crystal-clear answer to that, but the questions are definitively worth asking, every time.

The most important thing, in my mind, is to ask yourself: are you deceiving anyone in the process? Are you being transparent and truthful, to yourself and to others? Are you providing people with a genuine opportunity to choose freely? Do other people agree on your answers to these questions?

72. Consultant to Oedipus Rex

When leading and managing complex change processes, change agents often face the challenge of "speaking truth to power", in terms of telling the CEO something that he/she might not be pleased to hear. This happens because, more often then not, the current situation of any organization is, to a very large extent, the product of the CEO's leadership style.

Even though the CEO may have personally hired internal and external change agents and given them a mandate to change things in a certain way, that CEO may not fully realize that his/her own behavior is a major influence in keeping things as they are; the CEO may be the ultimate person to blame for everything that is not as it should be in the institution. In order to provoke change, the CEO will need to change his/her behavior and become a model for the desired change. This may not be easy or pleasant.

Sigmund Freud sought examples in Greek theater and Greek mythology to use as metaphors describing psychodynamic processes. Greek literature is indeed very rich, and it even provides a very nice example of the relationship between an external consultant and a CEO, through a section of the tragedy "Oedipus Rex", originally written by Sophocles. It goes more or less like this:

When Oedipus was born, a fortuneteller told his parents, the ruling couple of Thebes, that the boy would in the future kill his own father and bring disgrace to the city. To avoid the prophecy becoming true, the king gave the boy to a servant with orders to kill the baby. Instead of executing the order, the servant, who was an intern recently hired, takes the infant outside the city and leaves it to be devoured by wolves.

However, a couple of travelers on their way to Vegas find the baby and raise him as their own child in another city.

As we join the story, Oedipus has become the king of Thebes, after killing the previous king Laius. He married the widow, Jocasta, but at this point (SPOILER ALERT!) he does not yet know that the dead king was his father and that Jocasta is actually his mother.

The city of Thebes is suffering from a terrible organizational climate problem, morale is very low in every Citizen-Engagement Survey done lately. This is because many citizens are dying from the plague, a deadly disease that the town wise men are unable to explain, treat, find the cause of, or mitigate in any way.

Irritated by the lack of effectiveness of his internal wise advisors, Oedipus decides to hire an external consultant: he sends for the Oracle of Delphi.

Taking leave from another assignment to re-engineer the olive oil industry in Athens, the Oracle comes to have a power lunch meeting with Oedipus.

"So, tell me, Oracle: what is causing this terrible plague that is devastating my Citizen-Engagement ratings?"

"The plague has been brought into the city by an outsider, Your Highness, a foreigner who came here months ago. He is immune to the illness himself, but he has spread it and it is lethal to the ordinary citizens of Thebes."

"Who is this scoundrel? I must have him killed and thrown out of town immediately!"

"This, I cannot tell you, Sire. For surely you would be so angered at me that you would have me killed."

"That's ridiculous! Tell me who it is. I promise that I will not have you killed."

"Do you really promise?"

"Yes, I do."

"Cross your heart and hope to die?"

"Get on with it, man! Who is the cause of the plague?"

"It is you, Sire... You are the foreigner who arrived here last year and unknowingly brought a disease with you."

"What? That's the most outrageous thing I've ever heard! Guards! Seize this man and kill him!"

"But you promised! You prom... GHHKK!"

Like most CEO's, Oedipus did not like to hear that he was the cause of the city's problems. So he terminated the contract with the bearer of bad news. What was actually happening is that the gods were punishing the city and bringing disgrace to its citizens because of what Oedipus had done (killed his father and married his mother, though unknowingly).

In real life, similarly, CEO's are not aware of the fact that what they do, with the best of intentions, actually feeds the company's performance and morale problems. When they hear that, they throw the reports in the trash bin and fire the consultants who wrote them. Most consultants have learned from experience, so what do they do? They lie to their clients. They invent other causes for the company's problems, carefully avoiding to assign any blame on the CEO. By doing this, they live to get other contracts, though they fail to tackle the main issue influencing the organization's situation.

If you are a change agent, your main challenge is to provoke change without provoking the anger of the CEO, or of other senior leaders co-responsible for the sorry state the company is in. As Herbert A. Shepard put it in his brilliant 1974 paper "Rules of Thumb for Change Agents", Rule #1 is: "stay alive!" Otherwise, you won't live to lead another change.

If you are a CEO or senior leader, your challenge is to acknowledge that you have had a role in bringing the organization to where it is now; and if you want that to change, you will need to begin by changing something in yourself. Organizational change requires the leaders to change their behavior. Otherwise, they run the risk of being changed by the shareholders, who will remove them and replace them with different people, who will do things differently.

Oedipus refused to see what was going on until he was confronted with the truth in a way he could not avoid. He then gouged both of his own eyes out and wandered the land in exile, blind and unemployed. He was never featured in Forbes again.

It is better to try and change your behavior, avoiding Oedipus' tragic end.

Acknowledgements

I am deeply grateful to my friends and colleagues who first told me some of the stories featured in this book:

José Catuetê Borralho e Albuquerque
Rob Charlier
Juca Chaves
José Maria Velho Cirne Lima
Debbie Cummings
Floris Deckers
Maribela Faerman
Tom Fadrhonc
Paulo Finuras
Paulo Gaudêncio
Wilco Jiskoot
Robert Kegan
Jan Vincent Meertens
Rodolfo Nabhen
Geraldo Pereira de Souza
João Francisco Pereira de Souza
Mário Siqueira
Jô Soares
José Carlos Teixeira Moreira
Sunny Uberai
José Vasconcelos
Luis Fernando Veríssimo
Bob Waisfisz and
Huib Wursten.

I realize that I may have forgotten to include someone in this list. I confess that, as I am getting older, my memory is no longer what it used to be 45 years ago. Kindly refer to stories #13 and #61 and try to forgive me.

I am also profoundly indebted to my wife Jussara Nunes Pereira de Souza, for her thorough review and suggestions.

References

Hofstede, Geert et al. – "Cultures and Organizations" New York: McGraw-Hill, 2010

Lanzer, Fernando – "Cruzando culturas sem ser atropelado", São Paulo: Évora, 2013

Lanzer, Fernando – "Take Off Your Glasses", New York: Create Space, 2012.

Pearce, Terry – "Leading Out Loud", London: John Wiley & Sons, 2013.

Schein, Edgar H. – "Corporate Culture Survival Guide", New York: Jossey-Bass, 2009.

Shepard, Herbert A. – "Rules of Thumb for Change Agents", 1974. White paper available on the web.

Wursten, Huib & Lanzer, Fernando – "The EU: the third great European cultural contribution to the world", article available at www.itim.org

About the author

Fernando Lanzer started as a consultant over 30 years ago, but got sucked into one of his clients and became an HR Manager in a bank. Unable to find a real job, he was stuck in HR and in banks for three decades. During that period he worked mostly in Amsterdam and in São Paulo, where a series of bank acquisitions left him with 23,000 reasons for an ulcer.

Since 2003 he has been living in The Netherlands, where he completed 15 years working for ABN AMRO until being kicked back into consulting.

Fernando travels frequently to different parts of the world helping companies to cope with people issues in change processes, especially regarding cross-cultural differences, organization development and leadership development. He is also a former chairman of the Supervisory Group of AIESEC International, the world's largest student exchange network.

He enjoys red wine, coaching, writing, watching films, facilitating workshops, listening to music and public speaking.

Fernando Lanzer has also written "Take Off Your Glasses" (2012), "*Cruzando Culturas Sem Ser Atropelado: Gestão Transcultural para um Mundo Globalizado*" (2013), "The Meaning Tree" (2015) and "*Clima e Cultura Organizacionais: Entender, Manter e Mudar*" (2015). His books are available on Amazon throughout the world, both in printed and electronic versions for tablets and e-readers, and also at other fine bookstores and websites.

He can be reached at:
Fernando@LCOpartners.com

We invite you to visit his blog:
Fernandolanzer.com

See also his website:

www.LCOpartners.com

www.ingramcontent.com/pod-product-compliance
Lightning Source LLC
Chambersburg PA
CBHW070856180526
45168CB00005B/1836